WALLY OLINS.
ON B®AND.

WALLY OLINS.
ON B®AND.

with 55 illustrations

CONTENTS

INTRODUCTION

All successful businesses are made up of three strands: technical or craft skills, financial know how, and the ability to sell (call it seduction, although it's more usually called marketing). Generally one of these tends to dominate. It's pretty clear that technology is the dominant strand in Sony, finance in Goldman Sachs and seduction in Virgin.

Technically based companies take a deep pride in what they do. Their culture is based around the products they make and they continually work to improve them; it's their core. For many years under Henry Ford I, Ford had such a culture. Ford knew how to design and build good products by machine quickly and well. Many pharmaceutical companies were started by doctors, scientists or technologists who, using their technical skills, went on to build big businesses. And of course the ultimate technical businesses of our age are the ones created in Silicon Valley. People like Bill Hewlett, Dave Packard and their successors built companies which now dominate, or at least profoundly influence, our world. Bill Gates the Henry Ford of our era, has used his own and his colleagues' understanding of technology to dominate a global market place. So has Andy Grove of Intel. These companies didn't start up primarily to make profits but to explore, develop and exploit technologies. Almost inevitably, though, as in the case of Microsoft, they have matured into marketing and financially driven entities.

Strangely enough, many creative organizations, advertising agencies, brand development companies and other communications businesses, which exist to help their clients seduce customers, are technically based or perhaps, more properly, craft-based. Craft businesses share with technically based companies an enthusiasm for what they do. The people who run them are usually deeply and professionally committed. Often they are driven primarily by their own creative energy rather than any financial ambition, which is why they sometimes end up getting bought by WPP, Omnicom, Interpublic and other giants. By definition, though, what drives these craft- or technically based businesses is pride in what they create, rather than financial reward. Profit is the result of skills, in some cases almost a by-product.

The primary aim of financially based businesses on the other hand is to maximize their profitability. What they actually do to make money is secondary to them. All private equity and venture capital businesses fall into this category; so do most banks. Corporate raiders like the late James Goldsmith who move into businesses and strip their assets are concerned only with maximizing financial returns. Much of the breast beating which we have witnessed particularly in the United States in the early years of the twenty-first century about Enron, WorldCom and other scandal-wracked companies derives from the realization that if you give too heavy an emphasis to finance you may create a culture in which people start cutting corners and eventually get into trouble.[1]

Not all financially driven businesses are in finance. Management consultants exist primarily to help businesses become more efficient and make more money. Bain & Company rightly claims that its business is helping its clients create shareholder value. Many financially based businesses love what they do and are very proud of their technical skills – but they never forget that making profit is what they are there for.

The third group of companies is dominated by seducers whose rise to their current dominance is a main theme of this book. Serious books about business don't like words like 'seduction'. They much prefer, as I indicated earlier, the word 'marketing', which is fine; words are important. But we should remain quite clear that what marketing, branding and all the rest of it are about is persuading, seducing and attempting to manipulate people into buying products and services. In companies that seduce, the brand is the focus of corporate life. Branding is everything. Virgin is a classic example of such a company; its raison d'être is to win share of mind, then share of market. That's how these companies make profits. For Virgin and companies like it, what they do is not as important as how they do it, and more important still is how they are perceived to do it.

You can't run any business successfully without a judicious mix of all three strands. My view, though – and this theme runs through the book – is that seduction skills or, as most people prefer to call them, branding skills, are emerging as the most crucial of the three strands. Since branding is what I've been doing right through my business career I am bound to be a bit biased. In my experience, technical and financial skills equal to the best in your sector are mandatory, but you won't come top without a powerful brand. The reasons why are quite complex in detail, but simple in essence. These days because of the availability of the best technology to everyone, all the top competitors in any given sector are very good. In fact in order to get into the race you have to be as good as the best of the competition. This means that in most but not quite all businesses, technical skills alone don't secure victory any more. And if all the competitors are good, the one with the best reputation wins. It's true that in bio-tech, information technology and some other industries, knowledge and intellectual property still really count. It's also true that new product development and new technologies remain essential for any successful company, but in relation to the overall commercial market place, these activities, although very important, don't usually make a fundamental difference. Innovation is vital, but nowadays almost anything can be copied – usually fast.

As to financial skills, they are and always have been paramount and it would be silly to pretend, in a world dominated by the American business culture and the rapid rise of private equity and venture capital businesses, that finance plays any kind of subordinate role in business life. What's new, though, is that even financially driven companies now need image to be successful. Traditionally such organizations never needed to use marketing techniques; in fact they rather despised them. It's difficult to imagine giant personalities of the financial world like J. P. Morgan or Siegmund Warburg having any truck with image builders. Today, however, financially driven businesses are getting bigger, going global, buying up their rivals, and they need reputation and brand image just to compete. So while finance remains very much at the heart of business, it increasingly needs heavy branding to make it work.

In order to succeed, every organization has to have some people from each strand in important positions, but since their individual interests and priorities are often deeply antipathetic to each other, in every single successful company there is always an internal struggle between individuals from each of these strands for dominance. Very often the success of companies actually derives from this infighting: it's euphemistically called 'creative tension'.

So if the seducers with their brands are emerging as the dominant strand in business, is this a Bad Thing or a Good Thing for all of us? Brands have been heavily criticized. A marketing- or brand-dominated business depends for its survival on its customers' goodwill. Customers have ultimate power. If they don't like the product, the service or the company behind it, they can normally, except in highly regulated activities, go elsewhere – and they often do. If enough customers go elsewhere, the company generally disappears. Despite all their expensive, complex and comprehensive attempts to manipulate customers, marketing people will always in the end do what customers tell them. So customers need to be sufficiently motivated and articulate to tell businesses what they want and how they want them to behave. If customers believe that anti-social behaviour merits a boycott, then they will find that companies that are boycotted soon get the message and start behaving themselves.

If we want environmental sustainability, organic products, more pay and better conditions for workers in developing countries, and all the rest of the perfectly proper agenda that a small but vocal group of protestors demand, what is needed to get it is the mobilization of consumer power. In other words the answer to the question 'Is branding in business a Good or Bad Thing?' depends entirely on customers' behaviour. The future of the business brand and whether it acts in or against the overall public interest is up to us consumers to decide. This is perhaps the single most important theme in this book.

The anti-globalization movement has taken up the notion of branding in a big way, focusing particularly on the brand as the most public, seductive and manipulative manifestation of the corporation. That's why brands have emerged high in the pantheon of horrors created by the anti-capitalist, anti-big-business brigade. Naomi Klein[2] and like-minded thinkers have gone to very considerable lengths to demonize Nike, Coca-Cola and a bunch of similarly well known companies for, amongst other things, grinding the faces of the poor in Third World countries, suborning and subverting the education of children in the West, charging too much and giving too little to customers and potential customers everywhere, brainwashing people with relatively little money into buying products they don't need and don't really want and that might harm them, and generally acting like bully boys, thugs and profiteers. This may be an exaggeration of the 'No Logo' view but if it is it's only very slight.

I'm grateful to the design writer Stephen Hayward, however, for pointing out to me that the anti-globalists are actually not really interested in brands *per se* at all. For them brands are simply presenting symptoms of the capitalist system which sustains a grossly uneven distribution of wealth and appalling exploitation and waste of finite resources. Brands, they claim, are the chosen weapon of these global destroyers. Brands offer the illusion of choice, thereby creating more waste and greater exploitation of rare and declining resources. Further, brands only offer choice to people who have the money, level of literacy and information to make the decision to buy them. People who are poor – and that's most of the world – have to take what they are given by the globalizing, exploiting, profiteering companies.

These arguments against brands in commerce are not negligible, although they are certainly exaggerated; nor should they be dismissed as the ravings of a few fanatics. There is much that is wasteful and unfair in our world. And it would be absurd to pretend that global companies and the brands they use to seduce customers are only forces for good and that they never do any harm to anyone. But global companies do not claim they are in business for philanthropic purposes. Commercial brands exist because they are a powerful tool to help companies make money.

And we the customers in the richer parts of the world know it. Nobody is really kidding anybody.

The weakness of the Naomi Klein school of anti-capitalists is to treat brands as though their only manifestation is corporate and commercial. The influence, strategies and tactics of branding now go way beyond this. Branding is playing a large and increasing part in politics, the nation, sport, culture and the voluntary sector.

In Britain New Labour, reinvented and rebranded from Old Labour, won an election in 1997 around an entirely new set of carefully created, honed and manipulated perceptions. Branding is now used by the most successful charities, who know that a powerful brand can use emotional appeals to tug at the heart strings and to open wallets. Nobody would seriously suggest that Oxfam, Save the Children, the WWF or the Elizabeth Taylor Aids Foundation are sullied because they successfully use all the techniques of branding to go about their business. The key issue about brands, which the advocates of 'No Logo' either don't know, have forgotten or don't care about, is that the brand itself is neither good nor bad; it is how and where and in what cause it is used that's truly significant.

Today the really interesting issue about branding is that it seems unstoppable wherever it goes. Brands, whether in business, the arts, charities or sport, have become a social and cultural phenomenon with the most extraordinary strength and power, and what I wanted to write about was how this happened, its impact on society and how we consumers can influence what happens next.

I believe that the power of brands and branding will continue to grow and that it is therefore very important that we understand how we can manage and control them. I also want to explain how brands work; how to make and sustain them; why some brands succeed and some fail; and how they impact on the companies, regions and nations which build them.

WHY BRANDS ARE IMPORTANT TO **CUSTOMERS**

Brands and branding are the most significant gifts that commerce has ever made to popular culture. Branding has moved so far beyond its commercial origins that its impact is virtually immeasurable in social and cultural terms.

CHAPTER 1

PREVIOUS PAGES
**Aboriginal children
using a laptop computer.**

Once upon a time brands were simple household goods – soap, tea, washing powder, shoe polish, boring everyday products that were used up and replaced. The brand was a symbol of consistency. At a time of product adulteration, unreliable performance and variable pricing, it stood for standard quality, quantity and price. The brand's image projected and sustained the product.

Nowadays all that has been stood on its head; brands have come up in the world. Today we mostly take a product's functional characteristics for granted and while brands are still all about image, it is no longer just their own image – it is also our image.

Branding these days is largely about involvement and association; the outward and visible demonstration of private and personal affiliation. Branding enables us to define ourselves in terms of a shorthand that is immediately comprehensible to the world around us. Diesel, Adidas and W hotels is one lifestyle; Hermès, Ralph Lauren and the Ritz is another. You can mix 'n' match to customize, enhance and underline your own particular self-perception.

The brand is ideally suited to the age of the soundbite and the global village. It says a huge amount to like-minded people, wherever they live, all in one go. Brands were created by marketing people inside large companies to seduce customers – to sell products by creating and projecting colourful but simple ideas clearly, again and again. The mechanism of branding was designed for and defined by modern communication techniques. But the branding idea has become successful way beyond the dreams of its creators, even the most ambitious of them.

Branding has moved so far beyond its commercial origins that its impact is virtually immeasurable in social and cultural terms. It has spread into education, sport, fashion, travel, art, theatre, literature, the region, the nation and virtually anywhere else you can think of. Branding is increasingly employed by not-for-profit organizations and charities who compete in the emotional territory of people's hearts and minds with commercial brands for the money in consumers' pockets. Brands and the idea of branding are the most significant gifts that commerce has ever made to popular culture.

And that goes some way perhaps towards explaining that bizarre but everyday sight – perhaps the defining image of our day – in which people all over the world, from virtually every country in every continent, drape themselves from head to foot in clothing bearing the names and symbols of fizzy drinks, running shoes, cell phones, universities, football teams, skis, construction equipment or anything else with which they feel an affiliation. This is a unique manifestation of our time. It has never ever happened before.

Of course historically soldiers have worn uniforms to signal affiliation and clerics of various kinds have clothed themselves in vestments of hierarchy. Heraldry has always been part of any complex culture but it was generally confined to special people in particular situations. Today branding is ubiquitous.

The orthodoxy, of course, is that brands are foisted on a gullible public by manipulative marketing people working inside huge, faceless, greedy organizations. Riots over the past few years in Genoa, Seattle, Prague, London, Kyoto and elsewhere were intended to show up the multinationals and the globalizing brands they own as uncaring, deceitful, devious and fundamentally immoral. But apart from ignoring branding in the wider world, the world beyond commerce, as I pointed out in the introduction Naomi Klein and the other protestors also miss another fundamental issue. We like brands. If we didn't like them, we wouldn't buy them. It is we consumers who decide which brand will succeed and which will fail. Some brands are successful because people love them and can't get enough of them; nobody forces anyone to buy a baseball cap with the Nike logo on it. Other brands fail because people simply don't want them. They mean nothing to anybody. The only people you ever see wearing a Barclays Bank T-shirt are a few miserable people who work for Barclays and they don't seem to like it much.

All this means that the brand is not really controlled by marketing people, despite their huge budgets, their research programmes and their panoply of branding, advertising and event managing satraps. The brand is controlled by us – the customers. When a brand is really successful it can take off in ways and at a pace which bewilders those who purport to be in charge of it; and when a brand gets into trouble the opposite can happen. Look at Gap, which lost touch with its market place and tried to sell things people didn't like anymore. Gap has been taught a humiliating and wounding lesson. Or look at Levi's, once the uncrowned king of the jeans world. It's very hard to stay on top.

Nowadays we take for granted that a brand will function as well as the best of its competition; when it doesn't we ruthlessly dump it. The power of a brand derives from a curious mixture of how it performs and what it stands for. When a brand gets the mix right it makes us, the people who buy it, feel that it adds something to our idea of ourselves. Take a look at some well known brands. Dunhill, Church's and Johnnie Walker are primarily about being British, male, middle-aged and well-off. They trade on a kind of implicit, fantastical, never never land of Bertie Wooster, Sherlock Holmes and Hercule Poirot or Lord Peter Wimsey. Their strength lies in their ability to capture and make available something of this fantasy world at a high but not impossible price, to a small but large enough global market. Burberry, however, with identical origins has moved beyond all that. Burberry stands for something different. Thanks to outstanding and subtle brand management Burberry now appeals to a younger, more cosmopolitan world and of course a much larger market.

Brands come in all shapes and sizes; they may be specific or general, palpable or impalpable, global or national, expensive or cheap but in most cases, it's not just what they are, but also what they represent that makes them powerful. Pétrus and Irn-Bru, just to take two ends of the drink spectrum, have quite a lot in common as socio-economic, demographic and cultural indicators. They come from quite particular places; you can see them, touch them and above all open them up and drink them.

Both are about particular kinds of connoisseurship and aspiration. Pétrus is of course a manifestation of the scholarship and snobbery surrounding wine and has implications of wealth, breeding, taste and the finer things of life; Irn-Bru is 'Trainspotting' in a bottle; a caricature of young, deprived, Scottish, tattooed, drugged-up thuggery to which many people apparently aspire.

There are still a few brands around, even very big ones, where function dominates. Visa, unusually for a brand these days, is more about function than symbolism. It is so impalpable that it's a kind of wraith. It seems to have no provenance: it's quite as much at home in Turkey as in Thailand. It takes on the protective colouring of those financial service organizations with which it's associated. It is one of those comparatively rare brands that has virtually no personality and no socio-economic implications. And yet Visa, colourless though it is, is also one of those few brands that is now indispensable: we couldn't manage life without it.

Like many brands Visa has global reach. National boundaries mean nothing to such brands: they turn up in the strangest places, where they sometimes have curious social and sociological implications. Rich people in East Africa who drive Mercedes cars are called WaBenzi – members of the Mercedes Benz tribe.

Brands like Mercedes can sweep across the world. Their physical and emotional presence is ubiquitous, and they seem omnipresent, almost omnipotent. Disney, Coca-Cola, McDonald's and Nike use powerful, all-inclusive emotions to target a worldwide audience. They try to embrace as many people as possible, everywhere. A young athlete in the US wears Nike running shoes, both because he thinks they will help him perform better and because they are a fashion statement. Their purpose is both functional and symbolic. Of course most people who buy Nike shoes don't run in them at all – except for the bus. They don't even exercise. They simply show off in them. A cleaner at Banjul airport in the Gambia scrapes and saves to buy Nike running shoes as a signal to himself and others that he is able to share some at least of the rich world's glamour and fashion. For him the shoes themselves are much more symbolic than functional. The brand idea has made them iconic. When they first appeared in Moscow and Kiev, McDonald's restaurants had a similar symbolic resonance. They enabled the locals who could afford to go in them feel that they were connected to the rest of the world. Now of course all that's over and they're just boring old McDonald's.

Many great brands are like amoebae or plasticine. They can be shaped, twisted and turned in all sorts of ways yet still remain recognizable. That's why so many brands can be divorced from the products/services with which they were originally associated. The rugged, outdoor, cigarette-puffing Marlboro man now appears on rugged, outdoor Marlboro clothing. The relationship between Michelin tyres, Michelin green travel guides and Michelin red hotel and restaurant guides has on the other hand a certain logic. It's not that different from Porsche whose name, originally associated with high-performance sporting cars, is now stuck on to watches and a wide range of expensive sporting goods, all of which have a Porsche feel. This is called 'brand extension' by the marketing people who create and sustain brands. We take it entirely for granted, but logically it's absurd. Why should a cigarette maker be able to make tough outdoor clothing? In reality brand extension is a remarkable development, because it implies that the brand has a life and personality of its own and that, if the emotions surrounding it are sufficiently powerful, we will unquestioningly accept its functional capabilities. Brand extension, as Jean-Noël Kapferer, Professor of Marketing at HEC School of Management in Paris, says, is 'the direct consequence of the recognition that brands are the real capital of a company'[1]. What this means in the longer term is that many successful corporations are shifting their ground from making and selling to being – to representing a set of values. And this shift is so important that it is transforming huge chunks of business. This is a theme to which I will return later.

If a brand can represent both cigarettes and clothing at the same time, it shouldn't, I suppose, come as a surprise that some brands can even, by a process of osmosis, come to represent the nation from which they derive. Louis Vuitton, Moët & Chandon and Hennessy (despite its Irish sounding name) are all unmistakably products which are associated with and gain strength from an idea of French chic and luxury. These products come from LVMH, a company whose boring initials hide some of France's greater brand names like Guerlain, Veuve Cliquot and Givenchy. LVMH, now the world's largest and most successful luxury branding business, owns a plethora of luxury brands, many of which are not in fact French. Kenzo is Japanese at least in origin, Loewe the leather goods brand is Spanish, Emilio Pucci is Italian. With admirable clarity and objectivity LVMH exploits the national characteristics of all the brands it owns.

So the best and most successful brands can ignore or capitalize on their product origins and their national characteristics. They can compress and express simple, complex and subtle emotions. They can make those emotions immediately accessible, in many cases overriding mountainous barriers like ethnicity, religion and language. They have an immense emotional content and inspire loyalty beyond reason.

That's perhaps why Polo and brands like it appear to have a kind of spiritual power. In a sense brand affiliations seem, in our individualistic, materialistic, acquisitive, egocentric era, to have become some kind of replacement for or supplement to religious belief. James B. Twitchell, in his witty and clever book *Lead Us Into Temptation*[2], draws many comic, credible and powerful analogies between consumer behaviour today and the behaviour of individuals in a more conventionally religious era: the shopping mall as cathedral; the designer label clothing as crucifix, medallion and so on.

How can Twitchell, or anybody else for that matter, seriously suggest that brands of junk food and drink or running shoes have any kind of spiritual content? The key is emotion. Some of the cleverest brands, the ones that are managed by the people with the most sensitive antennae, are reaching out to create a relationship

LOUIS VUITTON

MOËT & CHANDON

Fondé en 1743

LOEWE

Hennessy

COGNAC

PINK

Thomas Pink, Jermyn Street
LONDON

KENZO
P A R I S

P A R F U M S

with society. Benetton has used conventional advertising media to project strange and often disturbing messages about life, death and the universality of suffering. Whatever else they are, those advertisements are not simply about selling clothes; in fact they aren't about clothes at all. They have social content. Benetton the brand is expressing sympathy for human suffering. Some people were moved, others sickened and still more cynical about what they felt was Benetton's exploitative and inappropriate publicity. In the event the company seems to have gone a bit further than some of its franchisees could stomach and has now modified its policy.

Currently as I write, the Gap website focuses on the company network – employees, suppliers and workers in factories in the developing world who make the product – as well as on the clothing the company produces. Tomorrow the website will no doubt be involved in responding to some other perceived corporate misdemeanour. This is not just a response to criticism that Gap, Nike and others exploit Third World labour; it's an attempt to be informal, open, inclusive and non-corporate.

Six leading LVMH brands out of a portfolio of fifty-plus: Spanish, Japanese, English and, of course, French.

Even Shell, one of the world's largest companies, and not traditionally renowned for its sensitivity to public opinion, appears during the 1990s to have undergone a Damascene conversion and now expresses concern for environmental issues. Shell, it seems, is attempting to recreate itself into a listening, caring corporation. Shell wants its brand, and therefore the whole organization, which the brand largely subsumes, to be respected, admired, even loved by all those who deal with it – employees, customers, suppliers, shareholders. Shell knows that its products and prices are no different from those of its competitors. Its only real competitive advantage is its reputation – being liked more. The extent to which a traditionally inward-looking geo-political organization which has very little direct contact with consumers can manage this is, at the very least, debatable. But you have to give them marks for trying.

At the same time as Shell and other commercial entities are presiding over the mutation of their brands into a social force, socially aware organizations, which are still sometimes called charities and increasingly social foundations or something similar, are beginning to mutate into brands. In 2002 nfpSynergy, a UK-based think tank, published a report entitled *Polishing the Diamond* on charities and branding written by Joe Saxton, who argues that a coherent, carefully managed brand is essential for charities and not-for-profit organizations. He is very conscious of the residual prejudice against branding within the charities sector. 'Each time you read the word "brand" mentally replace it with the word "image" or "reputation,"' he says, but in a cogent and on the whole well-argued piece he presents a case for brands in the charities sector that would have been inconceivable only ten years before. It's not perhaps what Saxton says that's so significant, as the fact that in the charities sector it is now being said at all. Saxton recognizes that prejudices against branding remain strong in charities. 'As one Chief Executive put it [to his Director of Communications who was leading the branding work], "I find this whole approach distasteful and contrary to the ethic of being a charity."'

In reality of course charities are ideal subjects for branding. The product that a charity sells is caring for the less fortunate. A charity's success is based entirely on targeting an individual's emotions. Do we want to give our money to the blind or to training guide dogs so that the blind are less handicapped in society at large? Do we care more about cancer relief or multiple sclerosis or aid to people in developing countries? There is continual competition between charities for our money. Christmas is the time when many of us most overtly have to juggle between indulging ourselves and our families or being truly charitable. If charities aren't about emotions, and therefore branding, then they aren't about anything.

Greenpeace, like any other clever brand, stands for a few simple values and a particular way of looking at the world, all expressed through a powerful visual presence and some pithy soundbites. But Greenpeace isn't alone. The Red Cross and its Muslim equivalent the Red Crescent are amongst the world's best known and most readily recognized brands and have been for over a century.

Amnesty International, with its investigations into unsavoury behaviour by obnoxious regimes, is an almost equally powerful brand. Over the next few years it's certain charities will become increasingly professional in their use of branding techniques.

As brands permeate the worlds around them, like charities, they also begin to dominate the companies that originally spawned them. Brands are often very much the most significant contributor to the asset value of companies.

Orange, the cell phone company, was originally owned by Hutchison Whampoa. It was part floated in 1996, then acquired by Mannesmann, then Vodafone, then France Telecom, which floated part of it publicly for the second time in 2001. Orange, which took a long time to become significantly profitable, is much better known and liked than any of its owners. Whenever it is bought or sold, which is frequently, commentators always make clear that its most valuable asset is its brand.

The brand has become so significant a phenomenon of our time that it is almost impossible to express any ideas, or even delineate personalities, without branding them. Even people who would shudder at the thought that they had anything to do with branding are trapped by it. Woody Allen's movies are as strongly branded as Disney's, although he wouldn't thank anyone for saying so. The plots, the characters, the camera angles, the music all characterize the Woody Allen brand.

In art Andy Warhol is of course a brand and Tate, with its sub-brands Tate Britain, Tate Modern, Tate St Ives and so on and its Tate Shop online, has become a powerful museum/gallery brand. Then there's *Tate* magazine and soon no doubt Tate solo retail outlets or shops. An interesting issue for Tate, as for so many other organizations that are mutating into brands, is that whether they like being called brands or not, the mechanisms and techniques of branding or reputation-building enable them to grow fast, get popular and successful. Tate admissions grew from 4 million in 1999/2000 to 7.5 million in 2000/2001.

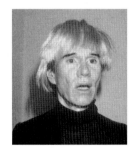

Woody Allen wouldn't like to be called a brand. Andy Warhol gloried in it.

What's Britain's most famous brand? Probably Manchester United. This soccer team plays in Tokyo, Sydney and all over Europe as well as on its home ground. It owns branded shops in Shanghai and Singapore as well as Salford (near Manchester). The club has connections in the US, too. It has a joint marketing agreement with the New York Yankees, it has a deal with Nike and in the summer of 2003 it is touring the US – all, as the *Financial Times* puts it, in the business of 'building and maintaining a brand name'[3].

And all this is new. Dostoevsky, Dickens, Balzac and the other great nineteenth-century novelists brought their characters to life through speech, clothing, houses, servants and carriages – never through brands. Zola, perhaps the most realistic of nineteenth-century novelists, would have revelled in brands, but neither he nor any other novelist of his period ever mentioned them. Even in his novel about department stores *Au Bonheur des Dames* ('The Ladies' Delight') from the early 1880s, in which he deals in the most intimate detail with every aspect of department store life, brands don't get a look-in. I couldn't find one single brand in the book, primarily one must presume because at that time there weren't many brands worth mentioning. Imagine it, a whole sophisticated department store world with no brands.

The David Beckham doll retails for £7.99 + £3 post & packing. In June 2003 Manchester United, perhaps unwisely, sold David Beckham to Real Madrid, which is a major self-inflicted blow for the United brand.

Today authors use brands to delineate a world quickly and succinctly. Even the incomparable Saul Bellow has created characters who live through and by brands. Here is Saul Bellow's 'Ravelstein' in Paris buying a jacket.

> *'What does this Lanvin jacket have that your twenty others haven't?' I wanted to say. But I knew perfectly well that in Abe's head there were all kinds of distinctions having to do with prodigality and illiberality, magnanimity and meanness.*
>
> *So we bought the jacket … beautiful flannel, silky as well as substantial. The colour was one I associated with Labrador retrievers – golden, with rich lights among the folds. "You see such jackets advertised in Vanity Fair and the other fashion slicks,*

and they're usually modeled by unshaven toughs with the look of rough trade or of downright rapists who have nothing – but nothing – to do, other than being seen in all the glory of their dirty narcissism." You don't even think of such a garment on an unwieldy intelligent man. A little fat in the chest, maybe, or with lover's handles at the waist. It's actually a pleasant thing to see.

The price was four thousand five hundred dollars, and he put it on his Visa Gold card because he wasn't sure offhand about his balance at the Crédit Lyonnais. Visa protects you from gouging; it guarantees you the legal rate of exchange for the day of the transaction.

In the street he asked how the colour held up in full daylight. He was deeply satisfied when I said it was gorgeous.

Our next stop was Sulka's, where he looked over the custom-made shirts he had ordered. They were to be delivered to the Crillon, each one in a durable plastic box. We then went to the Lalique showrooms, where he wanted to look at lighting fixtures for his walls and ceilings at home.

"Let's set aside half an hour for Gelot the hatmaker."

Pretty soon the usual Bellow things happen. Ravelstein dribbles strong coffee on his brand new $4,500 silk jacket, and doesn't even notice and then gradually, through the brands he buys, the way he treats them, and of course through the way he treats the people around him, the real Ravelstein emerges. If even a master like Bellow consciously and thoughtfully incorporates brands in his narrative to make his characters live it's pretty clear that they have a significant place in the contemporary cultural hierarchy.

When Saul Bellow, Woody Allen, Shell, Greenpeace, Harvard University, Scotland, Manchester United, Save the Children and practically every institution you can think of joins Coca-Cola, Burberry, Mercedes, Sony and a thousand others in employing either explicitly or implicitly the mechanisms of branding, it's fair to ask what branding is all about, and why it has become so compulsive. Why do we wear clothes with labels on the outside? Why do brands penetrate the entire world regardless of every other defining factor – nation, religion, social or economic grouping, culture?

Why are brands such a clear and unique manifestation of our time?

Simply because in a world that is bewildering in terms of competitive clamour, in which rational choice has become almost impossible, brands represent clarity, reassurance, consistency, status, membership – everything that enables human beings to help define themselves. Brands represent identity.

HOW VW, THE ULTIMATE CRAFT-BASED COMPANY, FELL IN LOVE WITH BRANDS

VW has put seduction, brands and branding right at the heart of its world.

CHAPTER 2

An unofficial VW/Audi sign in a Kosovo garage.

Adolf Hitler opened the Berlin Motor Show in January 1934. Anxious to make a mark in the social and cultural as well as the political sphere, he used the opportunity to express his views about car ownership. In the course of his speech he said, 'It is with bitter feelings that we see millions of honest, hardworking and capable fellow men … cut off from the use of a vehicle which would be a special source of unknown happiness to them – particularly on holidays and Sundays.'[1]

Der fidf Wagen

An idealized picture of a KdF Wagen cruising along one of Hitler's Autobahnen before September 1939.

Hitler wanted a small, cheap, reliable, practical four-seater for the German masses – a *Volkswagen*, literally a people's car. His Berlin speech was perhaps its moment of genesis. The prototypes were designed under the supervision of that renowned obsessive Dr Ferdinand Porsche, for whom the very best was never quite good enough. Dr Porsche was perhaps the ultimate technical boffin; his entire world was the product. Porsche had been brooding about this new people's car for years. He had made a variety of prototypes in conjunction with small, financially insecure manufacturers like Zundapp, but Hitler's blessing was his major opportunity. The new car made no concessions to contemporary automotive fashion. Neither were there focus groups or branding experts attending its birth – only Dr Porsche and his technical colleagues to whom styling was anathema, branding entirely unknown and function everything. It didn't look or behave like any other production car.

Because it was so uncompromising an engineering object, everything about the new car was unusual – its appearance, its air-cooled rear engine, the funny clattering noise it made, its willingness to cruise at 100 kph (over 60 mph) on the new *Autobahnen* just being constructed all over Germany, and even its name. *Kraft durch Freude* (Strength through Joy) was the name of the German Labour Front organization which sponsored the new car and was also responsible for hiking, touring, cruises and lots more holiday fun for the German labouring classes. The KdF Wagen was to have been purchased through a coupon scheme, but very few cars had been built at the newly created factory town of Wolfsburg when Hitler invaded Poland in

September 1939. The coupons were never redeemed, so even
in Germany the new car seemed a bit of a confidence trick.
In the outside world the KdF Wagen was regarded as a complete
aberration of no commercial significance. It was Dr Porsche's
ultimate crazy dream.

Between 1939 and 1945 the Wolfsburg factory built military
versions with some success and after the war the British army,
which found itself in charge of the plant, hawked the car about,
first to the British motor industry, which summarily rejected it,
then to Ford in Detroit which did the same. It was the car's various
unorthodoxies together with its deeply discredited origins which
nearly finished it off. No serious motor manufacturer thought it
had a dog's chance in world markets.

The ownerless and virtually nameless organization was
eventually handed over to a group of tough German production
engineers, accountants and salesmen led by Heinz Nordhoff,
previously of Opel. They persuaded themselves that its
functional integrity and simplicity had real sales potential.
Their determination was almost certainly born of desperation;
if the car had failed, they would have had no jobs. As it was, the
future looked far from promising.

By the time they had finally developed and marketed it, however,
the VW had become the finest product in its class in the world.
It was impeccably built, virtually indestructible and backed
by superb service. These remarkable qualities enabled the VW
to overcome its monstrous provenance and the unhappy
connotations of its more or less unpronounceable and rather
displeasing name. Over a decade (1948–1958) the VW
established itself as the world's most popular car.

In West Germany, its home territory, the VW trundled about
its mundane duties without a flourish. It was by far the most
successful of the West German motor industry's products and
motorways became full of the little cars clattering along for hour
after hour at maximum speed, frequently driven, as I recall, by

small old ladies peering near-sightedly over the bonnet. In Europe as a whole it was initially perceived simply as a decent, cheap, practical means of transport.

But quite fortuitously the VW had another virtue, of which its designers and manufacturers were entirely unaware. It had charm. This characteristic emerged entirely by chance. Nobody planned it in, or test marketed it. In fact it is doubtful if any of its progenitors knew what test marketing was. As a product the VW was guileless, innocent, simple, naïve, faithful and loyal. It was a bit like a dog. It is one of the more remarkable paradoxes of the VW story that a product with such an obnoxious heritage should, entirely by hazard, have emerged as a friendly, docile, ubiquitous, willing, almost animate machine.

The transformation of the VW car – that monument of technically based functional integrity – into the loveable Beetle brand took place first in the US. It happened, again quite by chance, that the little VW was the antithesis of the ostentatious, blousy, extravagant status symbols built by the US auto industry in the post-Second World War period. Perhaps unsurprisingly, when the VW was first sold in the US in the 1950s it became a favourite of American academics and the thoughtful middle class, the people who subsequently traded in their VWs for Volvos and who rejected the conspicuous consumption and waste represented by contemporary American cars. Put another way the little car became an ecological statement forty years ahead of its time. The car didn't just perform well. It said something quite clear and specific about the people who owned it, which is of course what all successful brands do.

Next it was taken over by hippies, flower-power people and other members of the alternative society who turned it into a different sort of statement. In a haphazard and unorganized fashion, having adopted it quite spontaneously, they went on to adapt it. They painted it in psychedelic colours, gave it a nickname – the Beetle – and eventually, as is the way of these things, sent it back into mainstream society. Disney memorialized the car with films in which Herbie, the loveable Beetle with a mind of its own, saved a family and their delightful home from the wreckers and a fate worse than death. By the time that happened the VW had become a Brand with a euphonious, charming pet name. So the Beetle became an American icon – a symbol of honesty, economy, thrift, modesty, good sense and charm in a sea of meretricious trash.

Did all this make VW management in the unlovely city of Wolfsburg happy? No, it did not. On the contrary, it completely baffled and discomfited them. After all nothing like that was happening on their doorstep, where their car sold on its obvious virtues. They didn't like the transmutation from VW to Beetle or *der Käfer* in German. They felt that the Beetle nickname demeaned and cheapened the car and might undermine its success. The idea of their product turning into a hippy icon simply terrified them. They were stuck with this one model, plus its van equivalent, until they could find an appropriate supplement or replacement; they certainly couldn't afford to see it sidelined or suddenly driven out of date by fashion. When I used to visit the factory as a consultant in the 1970s all references to Beetle or *Käfer* were banned. Their problem as they saw it was to replace the Beetle fast with something equally successful and then bury it.

The concerns that the VW management expressed about fashions and fads were very real but they were in a sense the presenting problem. Underneath lay a much deeper, more visceral antagonism and fear. Although they couldn't quite put it into words, VW's top management found the idea of marketing a product, even partially on the basis of its emotional qualities, dishonest, demeaning and dangerous, not only because it made them a hostage to fashion but also because it seemed to undermine more palpable, genuine and permanent product strengths. In common with almost all managements of the day they took the view that to win in the market place you had to sell a better product than the competition, at a lower price and with better service. And this was something you tampered with at your peril.

A rare photo.

You don't see too many pictures like this because we really never pictured ourselves this way.

For the past 23 years, while just about every other car company has been feeling the pulse of the nation and changing the looks of their cars accordingly, we've been fixing the inside of our little car just so you wouldn't have to have it fixed so often.

The result is that today, there's not one single part on a '71 Volkswagen that hasn't been improved at least once.

Recently, a top level executive from a big automotive firm summed up our position on the subject for us:

"Consumers today are more interested in quality, low cost of operation and durability, and less interested in styling, power and performance."

That's top level thinking? Our top level thinkers have been thinking that way since 1949.

That's why advertising focused on the functional qualities of the product, backed by the service network. VW advertising was very clever and there was lots of it. Perhaps the most famous US ad by Doyle Dane Bernbach sums it up: 'Have you ever wondered how the man who drives the snowplough drives to the snowplough? This one drives a Volkswagen. So you can stop wondering.' VW believed that the car sold better, because it was better designed, better made and better serviced than its competitors – and to some extent management was right. But not completely right.

VW was after all a North German automotive engineering company: image or brand or whatever else you cared to call it was something VW managers had never been trained to comprehend, let alone value. Implicitly they were suspicious of it. You couldn't put a price on it, or a number on it, or quantify it in any other way. VW managers were not untypical. At that time most companies which made products believed passionately that product superiority was everything. The brand – impalpable, unquantifiable, irrational, emotional and highly volatile – is never the natural bedfellow of the technically based or financially oriented manager. And that's why VW's conversion into a real brand-based company took such a long time. But gradually, as their dealers, their marketing advisers and their customers all repeated the same story, top VW management began to understand that the emotional qualities of the Beetle were perhaps valuable in promoting the brand. They arrived at this conclusion slowly, reluctantly and much against their instincts and corporate culture.

VWs don't break. DDB's advertising in the US emphasized VW's product strengths.

By the 1970s, the time that VW management really began to discover branding, the Beetle was beginning to show its age and the company whose fortunes were entirely based around this single product was desperately searching for its replacement. After a series of near failures now long forgotten, VW emerged with the Golf (Rabbit in the US) and the Polo which had been conceived by the Audi division of VW and of which Audi was especially proud.

The history of Audi is just as dysfunctional as that of its parent and a good deal more muddled. Before the Second World War

Audi had been a member of the Auto Union Group, best known
for producing under the aegis of the ubiquitous Dr Porsche,
ferocious, fast and dangerous, rear-engined Grand Prix racing
cars – competitors of Mercedes Benz. After 1945 the only bit
of Auto Union that survived was DKW; the rest was in East
Germany. DKW Auto Union, as it called itself, made some
excellent but expensive small cars in Düsseldorf. In 1956 Mercedes
Benz bought the company with participation from VW as a
minority partner. Then in 1964 VW bought out Mercedes and
in 1965, after a gap of 26 years, reintroduced the Audi name.
After a few more years VW also absorbed NSU, a small, technically
brilliant but over-ambitious company. By this time the firm
was called Audi NSU Auto Union AG. Not a name which
immediately rolls off the tongue. About the only remnant of the
old Auto Union company left were the four rings on the bonnet
symbolizing the four original Auto Union member companies –
Horch, Audi, Wanderer and DKW.

With a confused past and an obscure present, Audi was hoping
for a brighter future. It pinned its hopes on its new creation,
which it called the Audi 50. VW liked it and began to sell it under
the name VW Polo. For a time these identical products with
different names were sold side by side. Eventually VW realized
that this was a mistake and Audi, with great reluctance, was
persuaded to abandon its little Audi 50 to VW as the Polo.
Eventually VW calculated that it needed another brand to
compete with Mercedes and BMW and after much troubled
thought, including ideas around purchasing Porsche and
reviving the luxury Horch brand, Audi became the chosen
vehicle (if you'll excuse the expression).

If Audi was to compete with BMW and Mercedes it had to have
a personality as attractive as theirs, but quite different. This
personality had to be based around a reality, around Audi's
genuine capabilities. And that's how the idea of Audi and
advanced technology emerged. The process of change was much
slower, more hesitant, more tentative than it appears in hindsight.
Post-rationalization is a big feature of brand management. When

a brand is truly successful everyone involved is always ready to tell you how they planned it all along. In fact much of the time what happens is a bit of a surprise to everybody. But there isn't much doubt that both Audi and its parent learned a good deal about managing brands through the Audi experience.

As VW began to learn about managing brands it began to realize that a consumer's relationship to a brand is as much to do with what it makes him feel as to how it performs. These are easier lessons for an organization like a Prada, a Ralph Lauren, a Lacoste or a Gucci to learn than a North German engineering company whose entire ethos is built around product integrity and performance. I remember a discussion with a senior marketing man in Wolfsburg who listened to me as patiently as he could for as long as he could bear it and then told me that I was talking rubbish. You couldn't compare a car with a lady's handbag! The battles that went on inside VW as the brand advisers gained influence were typical of those that went on throughout industry.

Gradually, as Audi developed its own powerful identity, the VW range was also broadened and extended. The new products were of course far superior to the old Beetle which had been conceived forty years before. Despite this, though, and very much to their surprise, VW couldn't kill the Beetle, and it continued to be produced in Emden in Germany and at a plant in Mexico. If any of you has had the misfortune to sit in a green and white Beetle taxi in Mexico City or Guadalajara you'll know that even Beetle adaptability has limits. (Sadly, production of the car ended in summer 2003.)

By the early 1990s when the charismatic, high-profile and distinctly unorthodox Ferdinand Piech took over, VW had learned how to brand. Piech, grandson of the original Dr Porsche and married to one of the Nordhoff daughters, was an integral part of the Porsche dynasty and a brilliant engineer. Never a man to do things by halves, Piech accelerated the brand-building process at what some of his rivals and colleagues regarded as reckless speed. Under his direction, Audi became the up-market, expensive, flag-carrying brand. Today it's a deliberately understated, techno brand quite able to compete head to head with BMW and Mercedes both functionally and emotionally. With its TT two-seater sports car, Audi is harking back to the Auto Union racing cars of the 1930s to which it is, at best, distantly related and, further, to the Bauhaus, the most significant German influence on design in the twentieth century. Audi wants to be seen as the direct inheritor of the Bauhaus tradition; form follows function, and all that. All of this is conscious and self aware – contrived if you like. In reality the Audi TT is based around a quite ordinary VW Golf substructure. But the brand demands that the Audi TT should look like something out of the Bauhaus. So in today's Audi, form doesn't actually follow function at all – it just looks like it does.

The Audi TT. The ultimate oxymoron: Bauhaus styling on a Golf platform.

Nowadays the real daily contest between Audi, BMW and Mercedes and their competitors is about emotion as much as function. All three brands are good, they all perform well, although they have rather different personalities, and model for model cost about the same. In practical terms there isn't that much to choose between them, although they do feel a bit different from each other when you drive them. But it isn't so much how the cars perform, because the differences in performance are marginal although not insignificant; it's what they seem to stand for that increasingly matters. Image has become an important issue for motoring magazines to deploy. Even in the macho, technically dominated gobbledegook world of *Car* and its contemporaries, the brand is recognized as an extension of the individual's identity. Which car suits my image best? 'A BMW is for boy racers', 'When I sit behind the three pointed star, I feel good', 'A Mercedes is for prosperous butchers', 'An Audi is so understated' and so on. The real question now is 'Which of these cars gives me the self-image I want, and which in my self-perception makes people see me as I want to be seen?' So the emotional side of the battle has to be fought with the same level of tenacity and viciousness as the more traditional, rational side.

VW has now seen this issue with clarity and gripped it with characteristic rigour. Piech not only created a world in which his people are continually honing the image of Audi as an up-market techno brand, but they are scattering a lot of brand dust around other parts of the VW organization. VW, like its major competitors Ford, GM and DaimlerChrysler, is developing a series of brands to cover the entire automotive spectrum. Naturally there is great competition to buy up the best companies and VW had to go way down into the second division for some of its acquisitions.

Seat, established in 1950, spent most of its life as the neglected, more or less anonymous, Spanish licensee of Fiat. For a long time it made cheaper, older Fiat models for a local automotive market place in Spain which didn't expect or even hope for anything better. Under VW management, after a few extremely unpleasant, difficult and unprofitable years, it has turned itself into a quite potent Southern European brand. It is becoming or wants to become a kind of Spanish Alfa Romeo. Seat products bear a family resemblance to the rest of the VW family, but they look and feel more Latin. They are of course built in factories in Belgium and Portugal as well as Spain and they are made from a mixture of various components and sub-frames used by other companies of the group. Year on year, though, the Seat badge gets bigger and the front end or face of the car looks increasingly individual. Seat has its own separate distribution chain and appears to be carving out an interesting niche. Strangely, bearing in mind its profoundly dreary provenance, Seat is becoming exciting.

VW also invested heavily in Skoda, the Czech car maker, whose products prior to the VW relationship had gained a reputation in Western markets as a kind of shoddy bargain basement joke. Skoda now bears a family likeness to the rest of the VW range and seems well on the way to emerging as a durable, reliable, unassuming, high quality workhorse. In many of the world's market places the Skoda brand is now very respectable, even respected. To have turned both Seat and Skoda into brands acceptable in highly competitive market places is a major achievement. BMW couldn't manage it with Rover, which was in principle a much more promising proposition.

In the meantime, VW itself, the mother brand, has also grown and developed. The Golf has mutated over the last two decades but retains its original brand functions, appearance and personality, as does the Polo. New models and sub-brands have been introduced. The VW brand as a whole has steadily moved up-market just behind Audi, as Seat and Skoda slot into various positions below. For reasons which are no doubt emotionally based, because they don't seem to make much sense from a marketing point of view, one of Piech's last acts as head of VW was to commission a 12-cylinder luxury VW to be called the Phaeton.

VW's Heritage Beetle. Dr Porsche would not have been amused.

On top of all these carefully articulated brand moves, VW brought back the Beetle. Not the original Beetle of course, but a retro Beetle. The retro Beetle is a kind of Heritage Beetle. It looks like the original, only much more cute. Although the engine looks as though it's in the rear it's actually in the front, so there's no room in the car for luggage and not much for people. The retro Beetle is quite expensive for what it is and utterly useless for anything except feeling good, driving up and down and showing off in. It fulfils none of the roles of the original Beetle. In reality you could not find two products less like each other than the original Beetle and the Heritage Beetle. The original Beetle emerged directly out of technology. It was a functional product. The Heritage Beetle has absolutely no practical purpose and not much practical capability; it's a product based around emotion. It's very good for the VW company, however, because every Heritage Beetle is an advertisement on wheels for the VW brand. It's rather similar to a sweatshirt with a brand logo. The customer buys the product which becomes a poster site for the brand. It is a pretty, expensive toy which advertises VW. Like Queen Victoria, Dr Porsche would not have been amused. He might have been pretty amazed though.

All of these brands – Audi, VW, Skoda and Seat – are based around common platforms, systems and components. Like its competitors at Ford, GM and Toyota, VW has attempted to create the maximum number of permutations out of the minimum number of parts.

But all this is nothing compared with the next chapter in the extraordinary love affair that VW developed with branding. In 1998 VW acquired Bentley. Although Bentley had been a great marque in the 1920s and '30s it had been living on borrowed time for most of the post-Second World War period, even though it perked up a bit in the '90s. In the 1920s the Bentley was a Bulldog Drummond sort of car. It was traditionally painted in British racing green and it rumbled its way to victory in the Le Mans 24-hour race umpteen times. In the 1930s, when Rolls-Royce bought it, its character changed. It became 'the Silent Sports Car'. In both incarnations it represented the best that Britain could produce at the time. Now VW has created a new Bentley, a staggeringly fast, beautiful coupe with all the brand characteristics that during most of the post-Second World War period had fallen into desuetude. In this highly globalized world it shouldn't be a surprise that the new car was designed by a Belgian, Dirk van Braekel, who was also involved with the renaissance of Skoda. Bentley is also back at Le Mans – doing rather well, with a great deal of help from Audi, who keep on winning.

VW then announced that it was buying Bugatti, an ailing brand originally from Alsace but subsequently partially revived in Italy. Bugatti last produced a successful automobile – the beautiful Type 57 – in 1939. The engineering was brilliant and unorthodox, the coachwork superb and striking, the traditional colour French racing blue. Now a new Bugatti is proposed with a 16-cylinder engine – from VW of course.

In the old days Bugatti and Bentley didn't have much time for each other; they represented opposite ends of the sporting car spectrum. Ettore Bugatti is said to have remarked of W. O. Bentley, 'He makes the fastest motor lorries in Europe!' Bugatti in its heyday was as much the flagship of France as Bentley was of Britain. The heritage of the two makers is rich and very much alive. Very wealthy followers of both marques still exist in the US, Europe and Asia. Their supporters and drivers' clubs are both active and influential. Given the time, money, engineering flair and marketing creativity, these two historically significant and utterly contrasting brands will be successfully relaunched.

VW also bought Lamborghini, Ferrari's halting competitor, another brand that could do with polishing up a bit. In the flagship VW showroom on the Unter den Linden in Berlin, Bentley and Bugatti cars rub fenders with Seats, Skodas, VWs and Audis; the lesser brands gain lustre by association. With Bentley, Bugatti, to some extent Lamborghini, and maybe by the time you read this some other brands too, VW has moved into the world of luxury brands which have overwhelmingly cultural, social and emotional significance. This is not just cars any more; it's the world of Cohiba, Pétrus, Armani, Hermès, Burberry, Glenmorangie, Hennessy as well as Le Mans, the Mille Miglia and the Bauhaus, the Stately Homes of England and *le pur sang de Bugatti*. In other words these are potentially world-class luxury brands – the sort that new Chinese millionaires covet.

On top of all this VW has opened Autostadt, a theme park 'for all those who love driving' (sic) outside its factory town of Wolfsburg. Autostadt describes itself in a press release as 'a brand-new type of automotive theme world and center of excellence', a 'global forum of auto-mobility'. In this 'automobile city the general perspective of Volkswagen Group and the unique identity of each of its brands will become tangible in an inspiring atmosphere of creativity, individuality and dynamism'. So VW is also moving into brand experience, entertainment and the world of Disney. The VW press release goes on to say, 'The brand pavilions are located in a park criss-crossed by waterways. In their architecture alone, each is a statement of the respective brand philosophy drawing the visitor into its interior – the stage in a *brand temple*' (my italics). 'They [the pavilions] are designed to allow visitors to walk through and experience with their own senses the thoughts, dreams, wishes and visions of the individual Volkswagen group brands.' As usual when VW gets enthusiastic it goes the whole way. This is LVMH country.

VW understands that everything it does has to be coherently branded, including its factories. VW's new assembly plant in Dresden is a showpiece. It is the most beautiful car plant in the world; that's not much of a challenge, though. The flagship VW Phaeton is to be assembled at the Dresden factory where customers will be welcome to watch their cars being put together.

When Bernd Pischetsrieder replaced Ferdinand Piech as Chief Executive of VW in 2002 the brands were shifted around a bit but fundamentally everything remained in place, and Pischetsrieder has confirmed VW's commitment to branding, which is not surprising bearing in mind that as Chief Executive of BMW he was responsible for the decision to buy Rover.

VW is putting the most extraordinary effort into its brands. The group has not forgotten its roots. It remains one of the top car-building companies in the world. It continues to design and produce the best products it can for a given price and to maintain an iron grip on its dealerships. But it recognizes that the game is bigger. It now needs as much mastery over the emotional as the rational elements of its brands. The Japanese have been making cars quite as well as the Germans for years now. In cameras and other optical equipment Japanese industry has driven out the Germans. Germany won't allow themselves to be beaten in motor cars, though. Without in any way reducing their mastery of the technologies involved in car design, construction and service, German companies have to focus on something unique to them, something their Japanese competition cannot challenge – their brands. Attitudinally, this is revolutionary. It is inconceivable that any serious manufacturer would have thought like this until the last quarter of the twentieth century. Most have real difficulty thinking like this even now.

Is VW becoming both a Disney and a luxury goods company like LVMH at the same time as remaining a major automotive manufacturer? Maybe. Automobile design and manufacturing is where VW's roots are. And it's about 99% of what VW currently does. But as suppliers increasingly mutate into

partners and outsourcing in the automobile industry becomes more significant, the possibility that VW will become more of a design and marketing business – a service business – is quite real. VW has an impressive portfolio of well defined brands, some of which could move way beyond the automotive business. Both Bentley and Bugatti have the potential to become powerful luxury brands. And VW is quite well positioned to exploit them. VW currently dominates its dealers. It tells them what their showrooms should look like and how to sell their cars. VW will have to set up a new distribution chain with Bentley and Bugatti. It wouldn't be so big a step to make expensive cars the heart of a range of luxury products and service businesses – from hi-tech cars to tennis racquets, even to financial services or small luxury hotels in remote but desirable places which might be a bit of a challenge to drive to. It truly depends on whether VW is playing games or whether developing a branding business is deadly serious. The purchase of Bugatti and Bentley in particular, both brands with very strong national roots and a live, rich body of enthusiastic support, could lead VW to become a force in the branded goods business.

The new VW assembly plant in Dresden. Unlike any car factory you've ever seen.

The real issue is where this is leading VW. And the fascinating thing is whether VW can and will remain a motor manufacturer and move into Disney and Prada territory all at the same time. Since its deeply unappetizing beginnings in the first half of the twentieth century, VW has reinvented itself several times; each incarnation has been appropriate for its time and place. VW has always had an uncanny knack for getting things right at the eleventh hour.

My own guess is that VW is hedging its bets. It sees that the world is moving from products to services, that brands are at the heart of successful businesses, and it is experimenting opportunistically, enthusiastically and on a small scale to see what will work. Whatever the reason, like most powerful companies in the first decade of the twenty-first century, VW has put seduction, brands and branding right at the heart of its world.

WHERE BRANDS CAME FROM
AND WHAT HAPPENED
WHEN THEY GREW UP

Fast moving consumer goods companies
have lost the initiative. It has passed to
more innovative players with a better
sense for the new market place.

CHAPTER 3

So far as I am aware the first novel that was ever written about what were subsequently called brands was H. G. Wells's *Tono-Bungay* published in 1909. Tono-Bungay was a tonic or pick-me-up. Its creator was a small-time, failed proprietor of a chemist's shop, a typical Wells anti-hero. Edward Ponderevo is the archetypal company promoter – ignorant, impulsive, fraudulent, optimistic, amoral and with a genius for publicity. His nephew George, the hero of the novel, regards Tono-Bungay with a jaundiced eye. He doesn't attempt to conceal his distrust for the whole enterprise and his bewilderment that an entire system can be built on lies and greed.

However, despite his socialist misgivings, his contempt for the product and his mistrust of his Uncle Edward, George joins the business. He is clear that its success is based upon advertising. 'It was my uncle's genius that did it.... He wrote every advertisement; some of them even he sketched. That alluring, button-holeing, let-me-just-tell-you-quite-soberly-something-you-ought-to-know style of newspaper advertisement, with every now and then a convulsive jump of some attractive phrase into capitals, was then almost a novelty. "Many people who are MODERATELY well think they are QUITE well", was one of his early efforts. The penetrating trio of questions: "Are you bored with your Business? Are you bored with your Dinner? Are you bored with your Wife?"'

Tono-Bungay embraced every modern branding principle. It even thought global and acted local. It went into Wales with a 'more pious style of ad'. In Scotland, a special adaptation containing 11% of absolute alcohol, 'Tono-Bungay Thistle Brand', was introduced. 'The Fog poster was adapted to a kilted Briton in a misty Highland scene.'

Tono Bungay was also big in brand extension. 'Tono-Bungay Hair Stimulant' was the first supplement. Then came 'Concentrated Tono-Bungay' for the eyes. 'And we also did admirable things with our next subsidiaries, "Tono-Bungay Lozenges" and "Tono-Bungay Chocolate". These were urged upon the public for their extraordinary nutritive and recuperative value in cases of fatigue and strain. We gave them posters and illustrated advertisements showing climbers hanging from marvellously vertical cliffs, cyclist champions upon the track, mounted messengers engaged in Aix-To-Ghent rides, soldiers lying out in action under a hot sun. "You can GO for twenty-four hours," we declared, "'on Tono-Bungay Chocolate." We didn't say whether you could return on the same commodity.

'My uncle's last addition to the Tono-Bungay group was the Tono-Bungay Mouthwash. The reader has probably read a hundred times that inspiring inquiry of his, "You are Young Yet, but are you Sure Nothing has Aged your Gums?"'

Tono-Bungay was published in 1909 but it is set in the 1880s, when brands of all kinds burst on the commercial scene. The novel and the assumptions behind it are in many ways a realistic and straightforward piece of reporting. The leading brands, the brands that set the pace, were, like Tono-Bungay, patent medicines.

Patent medicines were the most clamorous brands, the most outrageous in their claims and much the heaviest spenders. They were the path-finders and the pioneers. The most lucrative market was the US. And what was one of the earliest, noisiest, most outrageous of these brands in real life? Why, Coca-Cola of course. The origins of Coca-Cola, still one of the world's best known brands and the model which so many others have followed, are quite similar to those of the imaginary Tono-Bungay. Like Tono-Bungay, Coca-Cola was started by a failed chemist, only in Atlanta, Georgia, USA, instead of Surrey, England. Tono-Bungay contained a little strychnine, Coca-Cola cocaine. The resemblances are uncanny.

Mark Pendergrast, a native of Atlanta, Coca-Cola's birth place, and clearly a man who has an intense love-hate relationship with his subject, tells the story of the growth of Coke and its less than heroic origins.[1] He starts by referring to the official story. 'John Pemberton, Coca-Cola's inventor, has been depicted by the

Company as a poor but loveable old southern root doctor who stumbled upon the miraculous new drink which he brewed in his backyard.' The official version of events is a myth, however. John Pemberton was not an uneducated, simple root doctor. He did not brew the drink in his backyard. More importantly, far from being a unique beverage that sprang out of nowhere, Coca-Cola was a product of its time, place and culture.

Patent or proprietary medicines were a huge business in post-Civil War America. Doctors were relatively rare, and often not very good, especially in rural areas. People ate too much meat and starch, which led to indigestion, bowel and other tiresome complaints. However, large numbers of people were more or less literate, had a little money and were quite credulous. Newspapers were rapidly gaining circulation. Transportation and distribution were excellent. All this was a fertile field for purveyors of patent medicines.

Pendergrast goes on. 'Patent medicine makers were the first American businessmen to recognize the power of the catchphrase, the identifiable logo and trade mark, the celebrity endorsement, the appeal to social status, the need to keep "everlasting at it." Out of necessity they were the first to sell image rather than product. Most patent medicine advertising was shamefully and flagrantly disreputable in its fake selling claims. Absolute remedial powers for cancer, consumption, yellow fever, rheumatism and other afflictions were widely claimed for preparations that had no efficacy for even the mildest ailment.'

So Coca-Cola was one of many hundreds of similar, semi-respectable concoctions launched with enthusiasm and exaggeration into a noisy competitive world. Here, according to Pendergrast, is the copy for the first Coca-Cola ad ever:

COCA-COLA SYRUP AND EXTRACT For Soda Water and other Carbonated Beverages. This Intellectual Beverage and Temperance Drink contains the valuable Tonic and Nerve Stimulant properties of the Coca plant and cola (or Kola) nuts, and makes not only a delicious, exhilarating, refreshing and

*invigorating Beverage (dispensed from the soda water fountain
or in other carbonated beverages), but a valuable Brain Tonic
and cure for all nerve affections – Sick Head-Ache, Neuralgia,
Hysteria, Melancholy, etc. The peculiar flavor of COCA-COLA
delights every palate.*

By the early 1890s it had given up claims to 'cure headaches' and
was simply 'delicious and refreshing'. Coca-Cola became the
largest single advertiser in the US. By 1911 its advertising budget
was $1 million per year, a staggering amount for the time. Where
Coke led, others followed.

Patent grain foods like Kellogg's and Quaker were originally
also promoted as cures for indigestion and similar disagreeable
personal afflictions. After a time, though, they were marketed as
cereals and Kellogg's stopped focusing on burping and belching
and became 'the sunshine breakfast'. In fact many of the world's
great branded goods businesses started as pretty dubious
enterprises – objects of ridicule and scorn amongst the educated
classes. It's a funny thought that many of these century-old brands
achieved such respect that over time they became more trusted
than politicians, lawyers, doctors, policemen and similar
traditional pillars of society.

The brands created by patent medicine people, which they in turn
had lifted from the age-old principles of applying marks of origin
to products, were copied by companies making other products
which went into the home. All kinds of household products –
soap, washing powder, blacking, shoe polish, tea, margarine,
corned beef, jam, chocolate, sugar, sauces and of course cigarettes
– were packaged and distributed to the new provision stores that
were springing up all over Europe and the US. These products,
with their consistent quality and standardized price, were
advertised in the cheap daily newspapers which served a literate
urban working class. The first great period of branding began
in the 1870s and '80s when all the technologies came together.
The great consumer goods businesses of the Victorian period –
Rowntree, Cadbury and Lever in Britain, Nestlé in Switzerland,

Henkel and Liebig in Germany, Procter & Gamble, Heinz and Kellogg's in the US – took branding out of the semi-reputable world of the medicine chest into the kitchen.

Many of the companies behind these brands developed into international businesses within a remarkably short time. Lever Bros., Heinz, the British American Tobacco Company and others became what we would now call global enterprises before the First World War. The brands these companies created lived largely through promotion. The genius lay not so much in inventing the product, or even in manufacturing and distributing it, but in communicating a simple, single, dramatic, frequently exaggerated and sometimes mendacious statement about it again and again.

A few of the great companies that created consumer goods used their own names on products, like Kellogg's or Heinz. But most of them – Procter & Gamble, Lever Bros. and the others – created brands such as Lifebuoy and Ivory with unsubtle but hard-hitting associations, designed to drive home the virtues and strengths of their simple domestic products to a naïve but literate audience. Harley Procter, son of one of the founders of Procter & Gamble, was, according to the company history, inspired to use the word 'ivory' for his new soap as he read the words 'out of ivory palaces' in the Bible on Sunday in church. Apparently the name was in his view redolent of the soap's purity, mildness and long-lasting qualities. Evidently, although Procter may have worshipped God in church on Sunday, he had plenty of time for Mammon during the rest of the week.

William Hesketh Lever was another soap tycoon. Lever came from Bolton in Lancashire, the son of a wholesale grocer. In his job selling soap, butter and other perishable commodities to retail grocers all over the north of England, he saw the standards of living of ordinary people rising fast and he felt that he could both anticipate and create demand through packaging, branding and advertising. In the early 1880s he patented a 'special packing' for fresh eggs from Ulster. He advertised Irish butter as Ulster Fresh Lumps, his earliest but not perhaps his most successful branding effort, and then he got interested in soap. If working people had enough money to buy increasing quantities of butter and eggs surely they had enough to buy soap. Most soap was then available only in greyish bars of inconsistent quality. Soap was a totally undifferentiated commodity ripe for development.

In 1874 Lever started selling a soap called Lever's Pure Honey. Then other grocers copied him and also started calling their soaps Honey-something. Lever was clear that he needed a soap whose quality was distinctive and unique, which could be distinguished by a trade mark as memorable as the product itself. Unlike his rival Procter, Lever was not overwhelmed by a religious vision in a church; he discovered Sunlight in the more prosaic surroundings of a patent agent's office.

The name Sunlight was one of a number suggested to him by a Liverpool patent agent, a Mr W. S. Thompson. At first Lever didn't think much of it; it was just one name on a long list. A few days later he fell in love with it and was 'all in a tremble to have it registered'[2]. At that time Lever outsourced production and focused on distributing and marketing. After a little experimentation – some of the outsourcing was poor, the soap changed colour, went rancid and stank – Lever eventually got product quality right.

From the earliest days, even though he built factories all over the world, Lever's emphasis was on marketing. He packaged Sunlight very carefully and expensively, first in imitation parchment and then in a carton, and he started to advertise it heavily. He later claimed, 'In the very first handbook we issued with Sunlight soap, which was got up by myself, entitled "Sunlight soap and How to Use It", everything was brought down to the level of a working man's needs.'[3]

In 1894 Sunlight, by then a roaring success, was followed by Lever's second major brand, Lifebuoy. It was promoted as a disinfectant soap, the enemy of epidemics and microbes. Then came Monkey Brand, Vim and Plantol. Later Lever, a man of pronounced megalomaniac tendencies, began to believe that he personally owned the world of soap. He took great exception to the Palmolive name when it was used by a competitor, in 1923 writing of 'the pretentious claims of the Palmolive people to a monopoly of the words "Palm and Olive Oil"'[4]. In 1924 in an attempt to destroy Palmolive he introduced Olva, which failed. It was followed by Lux toilet soap, 'the soap of the stars' – film stars, that is – which became a leading global brand.

Lever's company went on to merge with or take over other companies in Europe, the US and elsewhere. Eventually it became Unilever and went into every kind of branded business from soap and perfume to margarine, ice cream and frozen foods. Its brands, and at one time it had hundreds of them, fought with other global and national players to dominate the consumer goods market place.

Because it had a relatively small domestic market place Unilever became a global player almost from the beginning. Over the years its successes in developed markets were replicated in Egypt, Indonesia, Nigeria, India and other countries. In India Unilever's company Hindustan Lever became in effect the national academy of branding. In the years after India gained independence in 1947, Hindustan Lever, in a market of almost unbelievable complexity (fourteen major languages), communication difficulty and poverty, launched and sustained a whole series of national and global brands, including a major brand of vegetable ghee, Dalda, which in a very different sphere repeated Sunlight's success seventy or so years earlier in Europe. Dalda competed with and beat commodity products of varying quality in a price-conscious market with very low levels of literacy. Dalda became the leading *vanaspatti* in India and for many years it was the admired model which every other Indian fast moving consumer goods (fmcg) manufacturer emulated. Dalda's success followed the classic Unilever pattern. Product quality was excellent, pricing was highly competitive, distribution was ubiquitous and promotion of every kind from conventional press, film and poster advertising to village *tamashas* or fêtes, featuring Dalda stilt and stunt men and similar entertainments was clever and sustained. When as a very young man I worked in advertising in India trying to market soap, tea and similar products, Dalda was always my inspiration.

Unilever and Procter & Gamble of Cincinnati, Ohio, fought what was in effect a global Hundred Years War to dominate the household products market. The two companies detested each other and neither side was especially fastidious in its competitive tactics. Procter & Gamble had a much larger and richer domestic base, but its global expansion took place later than Unilever's. The two companies were pretty evenly matched, but when they went head to head Procter & Gamble usually won.

Procter & Gamble were great innovators. Ivory Flakes was the first soap in flake form for washing clothes and dishes. Chipso was the first soap designed for washing machines. Dreft was the first household synthetic detergent and Cresco was the first all-vegetable shortening. Without the slightest trace of embarrassment Procter & Gamble claimed that Cresco was the brand 'that changed the way America cooked' – and maybe it was.

The achievements of these branded household product companies were quite remarkable. Quite unlike the patent medicine people from whom they derived their marketing and promotional ideas the fmcg companies produced imaginative, innovative products of high and consistent quality. Underneath their self-congratulatory hype they really did manage to change deep-rooted social habits and customs inside a generation or two. The products of Unilever and its major competitors transformed and eased the lives of housewives all over the world. The new consumer products made life at a practical level much more pleasant. People washed themselves more thoroughly and more often. They also washed their clothes more frequently. They ate a more varied diet. We now live longer, smell better, have better teeth and digestion thanks largely to these huge companies who seized the promotional techniques that were invented by patent medicine companies and used them to market a wide range of what came to be known as brands. And they did this largely through unprecedented, unceasing promotion and widespread distribution.

Although fmcgs were not the only products promoted and advertised between about 1880 and say 1970, they were very much the most important and influential and they were the only products of any kind that anyone called 'brands'. What fmcg companies did was called 'branding'. They owned the world of branding. And the brand was aimed largely at the housewife. Specifically at the C1, C2 housewife.

Audiences were divided very roughly into the socio-economic groups A, B, C1, C2, D and E. As and Bs had plenty of money but there weren't enough of them, Ds and Es weren't really worth bothering with because they were too poor, so brand advertising for the most part concentrated on C1s and C2s. Within C1s and C2s it was of course the housewife who was the principal target.

Each very large fmcg company such as Quaker, General Foods, Henkel, Procter & Gamble and of course Unilever created an organization structured around the primacy of the brand. Some organizations had hundreds: global brands, national brands, regional brands; brands from companies they had taken over; brands they had dreamed up. But the whole point of the brand was that it only addressed one audience, the consumer. The corporation behind the brand was rarely if ever seen by the public. I once wrote, 'A brand is a wholly concocted creation that is devised solely to help sell a product and it has no life of its own'[5], and at that time that was the orthodoxy. There were very few corporate brands, or institutional brands.

And the managers who ran the brands were princelings. By common consent fmcg companies were regarded as the ultimate experts on marketing, and their marketing directors, brand managers and other cohorts were regarded as the fount of all knowledge about marketing and branding. They had big budgets and therefore lots of patronage. Brand managers inside large fmcg corporations would establish a pecking order based around how big their advertising budgets were. Their dominant creative partners were the advertising agencies.

Many of the pioneers of the branded goods business were, in the early days, themselves considerable figures in the advertising world. Pretty soon, though, specialist advertising agencies developed, in order to book space on poster sites and in the press – and to create advertising. 'Above the line' advertising was supported by promotions and giveaways of various kinds, described in a rather offhand, almost dismissive way as 'below the line'.

Packaging was not regarded as particularly important. Many advertising agencies created packaging for free. After all there weren't all that many brands to choose from and in a shop where the brand was displayed the sales person picked out the pack for you from the shelf behind the counter. In the 1950s the average grocer's shop only had 2,000 lines compared with say 20,000 to 40,000 in today's supermarkets. From time to time brands would be pushed through special offers, lower prices, two for the price of one, an extra 25% in the pack and similar inducements. Brands would tempt customers with special offers and giveaway items. These were called 'promotions'.

From the turn of the century until the 1950s, for example, collections of cards of sporting heroes, film stars, motor cars, or even characters from novels became major promotions, especially of cigarette companies. Liebig, the German beef extract company, produced some beautiful cards which have subsequently become collectors' items.

The media used in advertising evolved quite slowly at first. Initially posters dominated. Nineteenth-century cities were grotesquely disfigured with hoardings. Then the press developed into the leading medium, a position that was sustained over generations. Subsequently magazines using colour advertising became significant. In the 1930s radio advertising started to become important. Soap operas, that is programmes featuring domestic dramas sponsored by soap manufacturers aimed at housewives, were first launched in the US in that decade. 'Ma Perkins', a radio serial sponsored by Procter & Gamble's Oxydol brand, was launched in 1933. Then came cinema advertising and commercial

TV. Procter & Gamble's Ivory soap was first advertised on TV in the US in 1939, but commercial television advertising didn't really take off until after the Second World War. In Britain commercial television was introduced in 1955. So gradually advertising media became a bit more complex.

Until the 1960s consumer goods, everything from shampoo to lavatory paper, were the staple diet of ad agencies. It's true the agencies also worked for retailers, men's and women's clothing manufacturers, breweries, whisky distillers, car makers, banks, insurance firms and others, but these companies didn't have such big advertising budgets and they didn't have brands. It was household brands that really mattered and that set the tone.

Consumer goods manufacturers – the fmcg people and their advertising agencies – defined the branding idea. Although price and consistent high quality were important parts of the branding equation, emotional factors always dominated. Gradually research techniques were evolved and advertising became more self-aware and knowing.

Back in the 1920s the era of 'scientific' advertising had begun[6]. By that time it was no longer sufficient simply to produce slogans. The formula which advertising agencies had used for years to promote their clients' brands to housewives was now dressed up a bit and by the early 1950s it came to be known as a USP or Unique Selling Proposition. This pseudo-scientific nonsense was apparently devised by the American advertising man Rosser Reeves of the Ted Bates agency. A USP was the characteristic that made the product seem unique and of course uniquely attractive. It gave a spurious flavour of expertise and legitimacy to brand advertising. Curiously, even today, among the more credulous and naïve members of the marketing fraternity, the initials USP apparently still possess some kind of credibility.

In the 1920s Lever's Persil was advertised as 'an amazing Oxygen wash – discovered by Scientific Experts', a USP if ever I saw one and before the phrase was invented too. Palmolive, braving

William Hesketh Lever's wrath, told housewives that 'the After-Sting of Harsh Soap is the sign of bad complexion to come'. Ovaltine was 'the Home Beverage for Health' and so it went on. Much of this stuff seems to our more sophisticated eyes like grotesque self-caricature and its roots in the mendacious claims of the nineteenth-century patent medicines clearly show through, but some of it is still around.

As a very young man in the advertising business in London I worked on a Unilever detergent washing powder called Omo, which was advertised around the USP that, because of its magic ingredients, it was able to add 'brightness to whiteness' because 'whiteness alone is no longer enough'. For years, with very large budgets and considerable ingenuity, we managed to sustain variations on this drivel, or USP as we preferred to call it, including at the appropriate season the phrase 'a White Christmas alone is no longer enough'. And it worked. Housewives bought Omo in large quantities. And what's more I'm sure Omo washed clothes very well indeed.

Of course you can dress it up in all kinds of elaborate ways and make it sound complex, sophisticated and even dramatic, but in essence the USP isn't all that different from Edward Ponderevo's copy for Tono-Bungay.

Put crudely, perhaps a bit unfairly (but only a bit) the formula goes as follows:

(i)   This product is better because it contains x (secret, magic, new, miracle): the ingredient that will make a radical difference to your life.

(ii)   If (when) you use it, your home will look more beautiful, or your food will taste better, or your clothes will be brighter and whiter, or you yourself will look even more glamorous than ever before.

(iii) All this will happen with less effort from you.

(iv) Leaving you more time to make yourself even more desirable and loving for your husband and wonderful family.

While it was both recognized and acknowledged that top marketing expertise lay with fmcg companies, there were plenty of attempts to emulate their success. In the 1920s and '30s makers of radios, stoves both gas and electric, refrigerators, irons and all the other new domestic appliances copied the fmcg people. As families got a bit richer and more aspirational the ads anticipated and encouraged them. By the 1950s and '60s washing machines were being promoted. 'Washday,' said a young housewife all dressed up to go out shopping and looking over her shoulder at the world's least reliable washing machine, a Hotpoint. 'Just forget it.' Not too different was BP's campaign for domestic oil-fired central heating which started in the '60s. Mrs 1970 sat in an armchair in stiletto heels with her legs crossed, looking at her oil-fired centrally heated boiler and clearly feeling extremely pleased with herself because she had summer all year round. These ads were aimed at Bs, even As, rather than the fmcg staple C1s and C2s, and they hinted at a new world.

Another group of major advertisers were the automobile companies. For them there is no doubt that advertising was about selling. In the 1920s, in the US particularly, motor cars, especially expensive ones, were promoted in an extremely lavish and seductive fashion. Beautiful young women in cloche hats lounged across the impossibly long bonnets of 16-cylinder Cadillacs, while young men

Some UK press advertising in the 1920s – a certain style and originality.

sat idly in driving seats like characters out of *The Great Gatsby*.
In Europe automobile advertising was a lot more mundane. But
cars weren't brands. They were makes or even marques. However
significant all these organizations were, they all recognized the
primacy of the fmcg companies in marketing and branding. When
in the 1980s Apple wanted a real tough marketing man as CEO they
chose John Sculley from Pepsi. As it turned out, he was a disaster.

During the period between the wars, say 1920–1940, luxury
products like whisky, wine and perfume were quite heavily
advertised. These products were often promoted with charm
and flair, and many were beautifully and expensively packaged.
Clothing companies for both men and women in France, Britain,
Germany and especially in the US produced highly sophisticated
advertising emphasizing luxury, quality and (sometimes) quiet
opulence. Johnnie Walker whisky, Guinness stout, Coty perfumes
were all advertised with style and originality.

While some products and packaging were well designed and
promoted, some even witty, other organizations attempted to
project a corporate idea around quality and restraint. In Volume 1
of the British magazine *Commercial Art* published in 1926 there
is an interview with a Mr E. W. Decalour, the then Advertising
Manager of Shell, who seems to have represented this point of view.
'A definite colour scheme is of great use in expressing the idea of
uniformity. Shell in its earliest days were associated with a scheme of
yellow, red and black and this has largely been adhered to,' he said.

Shell's advertising in the
1920s: not crude maybe,
but not so subtle either.

Later in the interview Decalour goes on to say, 'The psychology
of the art side … is dictated by the character of the products; there
must be dignity and virile strength as the dominant note. Undue
aggressiveness is carefully avoided. The public have been educated
to a high standard by modern advertising, which owes its power to
a polite and cultured appeal rather than to blatant aggressiveness.'
Well, you could have fooled me!

'Shell took the lead two or three years ago [this is 1926] in the
abolition of garish and disfiguring enamelled iron road and field

signs and consistently endeavoured to get more artistic treatment for the signs applied to garages…' and so it goes on.

Although there were plenty of people like E. W. Decalour around, people who thought that 'good design meant good business' and that the corporation's public face was important, they remained very much a minority voice and for the most part they represented organizations who did not deal with consumers through brands, but whose corporate name was public currency. In Britain this kind of high-minded approach was exemplified by London Transport, which felt a strong sense of social purpose. Frank Pick, its communications chief and later head, followed by Christian Barman, were patrons of design. They employed fine designers like E. McKnight Kaufer and Cassandre on posters and they also worked with the best architects and industrial designers to create a public image that was 'uplifting', a word frequently used by such organizations in the 1920s and '30s. But of course none of these companies, Shell, London Transport, the railway and steamship lines, ever thought that they had anything to do with brands. Brands were, let's face it, vulgar.

They may have been vulgar but the fmcg companies that created them remained acknowledged leaders in promotion. Within the constricted, rigidly formalized battlefield that they had themselves created, the competition between fmcg manufacturers was murderous. In an attempt to dominate shelf space, they proliferated new products and kept improving existing ones. Watching their brands' positioning and personality closely, they tried to extend them into related areas and they spent increasing sums on advertising and promotion. The more successful brands you had, the more shelf space you took up. Easy, at least in retrospect. At the time it seemed very tough. Product innovation, both from new and traditional competitors, together with tumultuous price competition, kept the pace very lively.

And then it all began to change. Starting in the 1970s, a complex mix of interrelated, mutually reinforcing patterns emerged that completely overturned the rigidly defined advertising-dominated world of household products branding. Brands quite suddenly burst out from the narrow, strictly codified world in which they had been bred and over a period of a very few years became a commercial and then a cultural phenomenon of unparalleled force and influence. Leadership in branding, hitherto the almost exclusive preserve of household products companies, was snatched away from them and became the property of faster, more imaginative, more flexible businesses. Brands migrated from household products to retail to service to corporations themselves, and the media migrated with them so that now brands have become – whether we like it or not – part of the very air we breathe.

The L'Oréal strapline has evidently made its mark.

In retrospect we can see that there were probably five separate vectors for change. Each seemed independent of the others at the time. Now, however, it's possible to explore the massive impact that each had and to examine the explosive power that collectively they projected.

Not in any particular order of importance, they were: first, the shift in balance of power from manufacturer to retailer. Second, the shattering of traditional advertising into a thousand pieces and the rapid development of new forms of promotion. Third, the emergence of new media and distribution systems. Fourth, the introduction of extremely aggressive, sensitive and innovative brands like fnac, MAC make-up, Mango, Body Shop and Nike. And fifth, the fact that all this happened at a time of increasing and unprecedented wealth, where social, commercial and cultural habits dramatically changed and fragmented.

It's worth examining each of these issues in some detail. First, brands and their retailers. Beginning in the 1970s and burgeoning during the 1980s and '90s many retailers (especially perhaps the major supermarket chains) began to appreciate the power and influence they had over their customers and their suppliers. Gradually, as the bigger supermarket chains gained more strength, pushed the smaller corner grocers' shops to one side, and developed a strong bond with customers, they came to realize that they were able successfully to compete with manufacturers' brands with labels of their own. If consumers can be persuaded that Carrefour or Tesco dishwashing tablets are as good as and cheaper than manufacturers' brands like Finish, this represents a threat to the conventional pattern of manufacturer dominance.

To start with tentatively, almost apologetically, with cheaper and by implication inferior substitutes for manufacturers' products, retailers, particularly European supermarkets, challenged the manufacturers who supplied them. As their success and self-confidence grew, they moved from conventional household products like biscuits and detergents into fields that were traditionally quite distant from their origins, such as fuel and financial services. To do this successfully, retailers have come to realize that they need to create a consistent, clear idea of who they are and how they do things. If their reputation is strong enough, retailers are now beginning to believe that they can sell anything. They have created packaging and display material, and have even begun to design their stores to emphasize their personality. They now pay detailed attention to the behaviour of their employees. They fully understand that there is an inter-relationship between each of these factors, out of which their own brand is constructed.

At the same time as traditional retailers began to challenge their suppliers by building their own brands, they also began to appreciate their own power and influence to change the experience of shopping. It's all relatively early days yet because the culture and traditions from which most retailers derive is based around selling on price and convenience. 'You can park here and today's bargain is only $4.99!' Fun hasn't been a big issue. It's never been much fun shopping at Aldi or Asda. And Carrefour or Casino aren't a bundle of laughs either. But the idea of shopping as entertainment – a doctrine that was well understood by major department stores and that has been reintroduced into retailing by people like Nike and Disney – is now beginning to influence the major supermarkets and some are tentatively trying, one has to say with very varied success, to make their brands fun, although they find it very hard to reconcile 'fun' with sales per square metre!

If they get it right, and there are indications that they can, retailers are in a position to develop much closer relationships with customers than manufacturers are.

Second, advertising. As we have seen, the key to the massive influence which consumer goods manufacturers exercised over the customer derived largely from non-stop bombardment of advertising in press and magazines, TV and hoardings. The target audience was C1, C2 housewives, a discrete and relatively easy to reach group. The theory upon which fmcg advertising was based, broadly speaking, was that the more you spent on advertising, provided everything else like product quality, price and distribution were comparable, the more you sold. If you spent enough money you got blanket coverage and you could smother the competition. Media advertising was ubiquitous and inescapable. But as we move into the twenty-first century, it is clear that the old order has collapsed. In fact advertising has broken into shards. Satellite and cable TV have supplemented or replaced the main TV channels. There are hundreds of TV networks, some specializing in the most arcane topics. There are innumerable radio stations in every major market place. Newspapers are of course very powerful, and so are magazines. Even in this area, though, there is much fragmentation, with an immense proliferation of specialist magazines. In addition, many publications and TV stations are attempting to cross national frontiers. Direct mail of various kinds and in various forms is becoming more significant. Sport and music events, sponsored and sometimes even controlled by corporations and their brands, are attracting huge budgets and in each of these only a few global brands can be promoted. Promotion spend is moving increasingly into what we used to call 'below the line'.

All this means that there are so many channels of communication, some so broad and others so specialized that conventional brand advertising using blanket coverage of all media which reaches into every potential consumer's home simply does not work any more. So on the one hand traditional branded products are threatened by more lively and aggressive competitors, especially retailers, and on the other hand their traditional advertising base has collapsed so they can't reach all their potential customers anyway.

The third challenge comes from the new media. The ramifications of the IT jungle, the Internet and its various offshoots are only just beginning to be grasped. Although they were initially overhyped, there is some danger now that their long-term impact may be underestimated. Nobody really knows how important they will become, although there is evidence that distribution systems are changing. Retailers are finding it easier to deliver on-line than manufacturers.

But there's another more significant point. Conventional advertising is, for the most part, with the exception of a bit of coupon clipping here and there, passive; the new media are, for the most part anyway, interactive. It is the feelings and emotions of individuals as opposed to groups that are targeted. And that seems to have coincided with a sea change in the popular mood. Individuality, self-fulfilment and self-expression have emerged as major phenomena for our epoch. This demands an entirely different mindset from the traditional fmcg idea that if you repeat meaningless gibberish often enough a substantial number of people will believe you. It means that advertising and other forms of promotion can be more sophisticated, subtle, self-mocking, even ironic. It also means that the old and crude socio-economic groupings A, B, C and so on are no longer very helpful.

For me one of the most interesting characteristics of the Internet is that it gives individuals a chance to find out more about companies and their brands, and to challenge corporate behaviour and performance publicly. It's still quite easy for companies to hide nasty things – nasty financial manipulation and nasty behaviour to suppliers or staff, or customers for that matter – but now it's a bit easier to winkle things out. In addition people can now complain about bad service or mean behaviour on the part of companies, publicly. It's easy to ignore letters – harder to ignore the web. Websites set up by disgruntled individuals who are fed up with corporate behaviour and misbehaviour are a new and largely welcome phenomenon, even though they also encourage the green ink lunatic fringe. This phenomenon further underlines the decline of hierarchy and deference, and affirms the rise of the individual voice, which perhaps also helps to explain why brands which appeal to individuals as opposed to groups seem to work so well. Is this the post-modern society?

But there has been further migration in branding and this is the fourth challenge. Branding moved in the late nineteenth century from patent medicines to fmcg; in the late twentieth century it migrated once again. During the 1980s, while fmcg companies continued to play their traditional games, new marketeers emerged with very different and much more sophisticated attitudes to the customer. Benetton, Gap, Body Shop, Timberland, Starbucks and some of the others that I have mentioned were not just new brands; they represented entirely new ideas. None of them was aimed solely at the traditional target audience of C1 and C2 housewives. None of the brands used traditional fmcg techniques. Most of them simply ignored the division between product and retail; they were products *and* they were retail. The brand wasn't *in* the shop. It *was* the shop. And the brand was also the staff in the shop.

These new companies had very unusual ideas about branding. Body Shop hardly advertised. Starbucks reinvented coffee (some might say for the worse) and encouraged customers to lounge around all day reading the papers, like they had in a nineteenth-century Viennese *Konditorei*. Nike refused to recognize, or at least ignored, the traditional differences between above and below the line. What's more when Nike went retail, it built exhibition centres and monuments to itself. Niketown is not a retail outlet; it's a three-dimensional expression of Nikeness. Timberland is associating itself, like Body Shop, with green issues. Relationships between green brands that sell things, like Body Shop, and green brands that purport to save the world, like Greenpeace, are getting close. These brands take over huge international events. In other words they have created their own media. Above all they target individuals, not socio-economic groups.

These new brands blew holes into the traditional marketing/ branding business. But it didn't stop here. Brands migrated once again – this time into services. In the 1990s the service business, led by a combination of IT and deregulation, went into explosive growth. The service sector had been growing very rapidly for years and all the statistics in every advanced country show a relative decline in manufacturing and a growth in services from the mid-1970s. But the deregulation of financial services and telecoms, water and other utilities, combined with developments in information technology, led to the growth of entirely new, highly competitive activity in service businesses.

Service businesses are now massive brand-builders. Some of the biggest companies in the world are now service companies of one kind or another. IT blurs borders with telecoms to produce an entirely new business built around infocoms. There were 178 phone companies in Britain in 2000 compared with one in 1980. The competition between them and the ingenuity they have to demonstrate means that they have now taken over the lead in branding from fmcg businesses. Many of the new service businesses like ish in Germany fail, but when they win, like Orange, they win big.

Financial service institutions, which were an oligopoly in most countries until only a few years ago, are now more or less entirely free to sell any financial product anywhere using any distribution system they feel like. So all the major banks, insurance companies and mortgage companies are promoting themselves both under their traditional names and under new brand names in new and traditional media. Many of these brands, like Egg and First Direct, are highly innovative and because they have lower overheads they can offer more competitive pricing. All over the world financial service businesses are merging, throwing up brands in every corner of the market place. They are competing in a frenzy on every front. Most don't deliver well – yet. But in mitigation one has to say it's still pretty new.

Then there's the fifth factor. The overwhelming changes in branding have taken place at a time when in Europe, the US and great chunks of Asia wealth on an unprecedented scale has completely changed the way many people live and think. The state has retreated, private enterprise has expanded and individuals are becoming much more sceptical about established institutions like the police, the medical profession and the political world. Brands which are lively, personal, adaptable and seem to embody this new spirit are attractive.

All this is very bad news for fmcg companies which once shaped the idea of branding. They have lost the initiative. It has passed to more innovative players with a better sense for the new market place. In September 2000 the *Financial Times* described the world's consumer goods companies as 'dismayed, unloved and not a little frightened'[7]. Their stock market price has plunged. The best people from the best graduate management schools aren't interested in selling Harpic; they want to join investment banks and rule the world. What's more, fmcgs are a convenient, easy and high-profile target for the anti-globalization, anti-capitalist movement.

Naturally fmcg companies are trying hard to fight back. Unilever, always game for a fight, is struggling to get into services. Myhome, now rebranded Chores, is a home-cleaning service. Cha was established as a chain of tea houses. Unilever and its competitors are also working hard on building businesses in China, Russia and other developing markets, where the social and cultural climates remain far more receptive to their traditional ways of operating. Nobody should think of writing the fmcg companies off. They have great strengths, but the baton of brand leadership has passed.

Nevertheless there's life in the old dog yet – and the fmcgs certainly haven't lost their traditional chutzpah. Snapple, a classic kids' brand which has been owned by at least three companies over a five-year period and which owes much more to the chemist's laboratory than nature for its ingredients, has a wonderful USP: it claims to be 'made from the best stuff on earth'. Is Snapple a direct descendant of Tono Bungay, 'a mischievous trash, slightly stimulating, aromatic and attractive'? Probably! You can't keep a good USP down.

LIVING THE BRAND
MANAGING SERVICE BRANDS

In the future the model for brand management in a service business may be the British Army's SAS or the Brazilian soccer squad rather than Fairy Liquid dishwashing detergent.

CHAPTER 4

Iberia, the Spanish airline, once lost my younger daughter. She was twelve and was flying back to London from Spain unaccompanied, but because of an oversight, or because the cabin crew couldn't be bothered, Iberia mislaid her. She boarded the plane in Malaga, my wife and I knew that, but she didn't appear at the London end. After an hour or so, we became quite frantic. Eventually she turned up at the wrong terminal. Some passengers on the plane had befriended her and guided her out. Of course she rather wondered what all the fuss was about. We were terribly upset and tried to get some sense out of the airline. I never got an apology from Iberia and their explanations were muddled, senseless and contradictory. It was all somebody else's fault – nothing to do with them.

Iberia press advertising, 2002, focuses on looking after children!

Eventually I wrote to the chairman asking him what he would feel in similar circumstances. I got no reply, no doubt because he was too busy making a speech about the importance of service management in the airline business. Bearing in mind their 2002 advertising, with its focus on children, one might really expect a better performance. Needless to say, I have never forgiven Iberia, and I will never fly on it again unless I have absolutely no option.

That's just one story. I've got plenty. So have we all. Airlines who turn us away when we have valid tickets, cell phone companies who won't let us call from abroad when we're properly cleared, banks who lose our money then charge us for finding it. My most recent nightmare is from Omega, Securicor's parcel delivery service, now sold to Deutsche Post. The website is a gem of business drivel:

> *You want expertise, professionalism and value for money. A company that understands all your distribution needs, however complex, and one that offers totally integrated distribution solutions.*
>
> *Securicor Omega Express is that company. We offer a comprehensive range of Sameday, Nextday and European services dedicated to meeting your needs through an extensive door to door network spanning the UK and Europe.*

Our customers are the key to our success and our commitment is to maintain the highest possible standards of service in every aspect of our business.

Our forward looking and dynamic approach means we never stand still; we constantly review and develop our services to match customer needs and expectations. Stringent selection procedures and dedicated training facilities ensure the highest standards of competency and integrity in all our employees.

The creative use of Information Technology is vital in maintaining a competitive edge. Customers of Securicor Omega Express benefit from an ongoing investment programme in leading edge IT. Automated parcel sortation using bar codes and high speed laser scanning, optical storage of proof of delivery information and the latest Track and Trace *technology combine to provide accurate and timely management information.*

I thought you might like to read that bland soggy pap, because my most recent experience of Omega's creative use of Information Technology is that they will not give a time slot or even indicate whether they will deliver a parcel in the morning or afternoon. Why? Because, to quote from one of the 'highly trained, stringently selected employees' based in Omega's Newbury office, 'There may be a traffic jam and we'll get held up.' On this particular occasion I was disappointed but not especially surprised to observe that she failed to demonstrate 'the highest standards of competency' which the website had led me to expect. Nor apparently has Securicor's 'creative use of Information Technology' yet advanced to the stage where their delivery drivers seem able to use the cell phone. That's why, despite their 'forward looking and dynamic approach', I had to stay at home all day waiting for them to deliver. Securicor or Omega or whatever it is they call themselves are in my experience appalling but unhappily they are about par for the course.

It's absolutely endless. While most product brands are more or less OK, service brands mostly remain pretty awful. Why? It's simply that despite all the hype, corporations still have very little real understanding of what it takes to manage a service brand and they still use consumer product branding as their role model.

As everybody knows, branding began with consumer products. The whole idea was to produce consistent quality and standard pricing in a range of ordinary household goods, which had up till then been subject to adulteration; plenty of dirty water and chalk in the milk and a lot of brick dust in the jam. It wasn't easy to persuade consumers to trust brands, but in the end it happened. Now we absolutely take for granted that the branded products we buy will work, that they won't harm us – even if they don't do us quite as much good as they claim. Of course it's true that at the cutting edge of IT, biotech and pharmaceuticals, mistakes are made; there's the genetically modified products scare, and it may well be the case that junk food really is just that but despite that, most of the time we don't have that much to complain about in the branded products we buy.

The story in services is quite different. You don't have to look far. Wait in the freezing cold hour after hour till a breakdown service vehicle eventually arrives to look after your wounded car, or ask yourself why banks are for the most part a byword for greedy incompetence, or why your cell phone company doesn't know how to answer the phone. Service brands are very often badly managed. The reason is that managing service brands appears to be a discipline that is misunderstood by most orthodox marketing people. They seem unable to grasp its real implications. Traditional marketing people were brought up with products. Once the product has been researched, designed, made and prepared for production it won't go wrong. You can make it by the hundred or the thousand or the million and it won't change: one pack of Wrigley's gum is much like another, and the experience of chewing gum doesn't change much.

Service brands, on the other hand, rely on people, therefore each individual transaction is different. Until a few years ago most service businesses were either quite tiny like the local plumber, monopolistic like gas, water, electricity and phone utilities, or oligopolistic like airlines, banks and insurance companies. These organizations didn't think too much about service – they didn't need to, there wasn't much competition – so we the customers more or less had to take what we were given. Then suddenly from the mid-1980s onwards the combination of deregulation, globalization and new technologies changed everything and service brands burst onto the marketing scene. Now most services are heavily branded, heavily promoted and in some ways becoming more important than products in our lives. But the attempt to manage service brands as though they were product brands has created catastrophe.

Kit Kat doesn't answer back, doesn't get tired, isn't anxious, is always ready to perform and always tastes the same. Service brands aren't like that. People who represent the organization lose their tempers, get tired and anxious, and sometimes have just had enough that day. Call centres are staffed with people, not ice cream. And that is what makes service branding so much harder and more complex to manage than product branding. Product brands are about products. Service brands are about people.

Of course, as we all know, traditional product marketing depends on understanding customers, on getting a feeling for what people will be prepared to buy or want to possess. But marketing service brands demands an additional skill, getting your own staff to love the brand and to live it and breathe it so that they can become the personal manifestation of the brand when they deal with customers.

In order to get an effective service brand, people have to be taught to live the brand they work with. For the customer, the person who represents the brand *is* the brand. If he or she doesn't perform properly, the relationship between the brand and the customer may collapse. The skills required to teach staff to live the brand have much more in common with managing people than with conventional marketing management.

That's why with a product brand you can spend 75% of your time, money and energy trying to influence customers and 25% on everything else, while with a service brand you have to spend at least 50% of your time and money influencing your own people. The priorities are the other way round. In a product brand, customers come first. But in a service brand, your own people come first.

Increasingly, though, product brands are acquiring service elements. Service issues have emerged even in businesses that on the face of it appear to be entirely product-focused. Look at aero engines, for instance. In the aero engine business at first sight, hardware is everything: you couldn't find a business more firmly based around a product. If Rolls-Royce engines don't perform as well as GE's, they're out. There is not much room for sentiment or emotion. Aero engines are the ultimate performance-based hardware business. Or are they? Nowadays, assuming one manufacturer's engine performs as well as another, and they usually do, and financing arrangements are similar, the big issue around an aero engine sale is service. What the airlines want to know is, how many flying hours between servicing? How quickly can spares be sent? How easily can they be fitted? What guarantees does the engine manufacturer give about down time? How many service locations are there in the world? How fast will they respond? Which aero engine manufacturer gives the best service? What are his people like? Are they quick, helpful and responsive, or are they surly and bureaucratic? In other words, even in this apparently most product-dominated of worlds, service really matters and it often makes the difference between winning and losing a contract.

Service really matters in pharmaceuticals too. Although doctors are supposed to read their medical journals to keep up to date with new developments, they rely increasingly on medical representatives, the people who visit them from pharmaceutical companies, to learn what's going on. Doctors' views on the different and competing pharmaceutical companies are influenced by what they think of the representatives who visit them, not to speak of conferences and similar 'oh be joyfuls' helpfully arranged by the pharmaceutical companies. In this sense pharmaceuticals is as much a service as a product business.

It's similar with car and truck builders and for that matter practically every other kind of equipment manufacturer. There was a time, not so very long ago, when automobile makers were only concerned with what they made, and how much of it. They weren't remotely interested in what happened to their product afterwards. Service was something that was left to dealers. And dealers had a curious quasi-independent status. Their job was to sell cars and service them afterwards, so inevitably they represented the face of the automobile maker to the public, and what an unpleasant, unreliable face it so often was!

Gradually, car makers began to understand that buying a car was just one negotiation, but repeat purchases depended largely on how dealers performed. So automobile companies learned to exercise more control over the dealer. Nowadays they design dealers' premises, show them how to display cars, teach them how to service them and how to behave with customers. They attempt to turn dealers into a personal and direct manifestation of themselves in relation to customers. Automobile makers have no alternative if they want a close relationship with people who buy and use their products. Eventually the customer looks at the car not only as a product, but as a package of product and service. This kind of thinking is quite hard for an organization that has spent its entire life making products. It requires a massive change in the culture of the organization, but they have to do it.

There are, however, some sectors where the balance between product and service is heavily biased towards service in the first place. Take a cell phone brand. Since all cell phone services use the same hardware, customers can't tell much about their particular phone brand from the product, the Nokia or Motorola they hold in their hands. Communications – that is, advertising and promotion – are of course very important in creating the ethos of the brand. The brand makes its emotional claims through advertising: 'The future's bright, the future's Orange.'

But in a service brand behaviour is overwhelmingly important for the customer because that is the only way by which he or she can judge whether the brand lives up to the claims it makes in its communications. Is the future genuinely brighter with Orange? Is Orange actually a nicer, more pleasant, easier brand to live with than the competition? The only way to find out is to look at what happens when you use the brand in your daily life – and especially when things go wrong, which, inevitably, sooner or later, they will. That's the time that the service brand gets judged. When things don't work properly, how does the brand respond? Well, the brand's response depends entirely on its people. They are the brand. Do they lie, pass the buck, keep you waiting interminably, lose your reference number, move you from one endless phone waiting period to another? In that case it's a lousy brand. Or are they helpful and quick and friendly and sympathetic? And do they act on your behalf to put things right? In that case it's an excellent brand. In both cases it's the people and how they are trained to behave that represent the brand. In the service brand business, communications makes the brand claims but behaviour confirms or denies them.

Cell phone businesses are new. They are feeling their way; none of them are mature. One or two, however, stand out as brands that have the right emphasis, that understand that coherent, consistent behaviour of staff is the key to making a successful service brand in the longer term.

Ocado is a supermarket on-line delivery service. It's the bright idea of two young investment bankers from Goldman Sachs working with Waitrose. As I write it's a pilot scheme operating in London and the near out-of-town. Ocado makes the same claims as every other on-line retailer – and the same mistakes. The difference is that they get rectified fast, because Ocado don't use drivers of delivery trucks to deliver, but people who have been trained in service businesses, such as former British Airways stewards. So instead of uttering monosyllabic grunts when a mistake is made, the delivery person actually tries to deal with the issue. The people behind Ocado seem genuinely to understand service and are making real efforts to make the brand work.

Banks were created around the idea of individual relationships with the customer. Retail banks long ago established a network of branches, each with its own manager. The bank manager, a pillar of society, the very personification of integrity and good sense, established the closest relationships with his local community, and in that way the bank became part of it. All this represented everything that the very best service brands currently aspire to. Until the middle of the twentieth century banks didn't, of course, think of themselves as brands; the idea would have horrified them. They hardly thought of themselves as wholly commercial entities. They didn't even compete with each other for business, not overtly anyway or, as a senior banker said to me in the early 1970s, 'I don't like my people touting for business. It's vulgar.' Their products were, as indeed they still are, more or less commoditized; their branches were designed to be imposing and conservative; their communications were ponderous and patronising; but they were also amicable without being intimate. The real strength of banks lay in the behaviour of their people – especially those rocks of probity, their branch managers. Branch managers carried out the marketing policy of the organization. They were respected, cautious, careful, helpful, accurate. Banks were, without knowing it, classic service brands of a particular type.

Well, all that has been swept away and is now barely remembered even by the longest serving employees. Now banks are no longer respected; indeed in many countries they are hugely distrusted. How did it happen? What went wrong? Back in the 1970s banks began tentatively to compete for business. Then with deregulation in the '80s and the opportunity to sell a wide range of financial products, insurance, mortgages and so on, the competition got rougher. Banks began to merge. British retail banking is typical of much banking practice and behaviour all over Europe. In the US the pattern is a little different because of legal restrictions. But just as an example let's look at the UK banking experience. Sometimes, as British banks began to merge, they found themselves with two or even three branches in the High Street and they had to close some down. As the commercial climate got tougher and banks began to compete with all the other financial institutions who sold similar products, they started to cut corners, charge for services they'd previously given away and try even harder to get customers.

New technology enabled banks to do things much more economically than before because it reduced the need for staff. If you're a bank, competition is tough and you want to make a lot of money to satisfy shareholders, deter takeover bids and maybe do a bit of taking over yourself, the obvious thing to do is close branches and automate everything within sight. This brings massive economies. At the same time you begin to charge for everything you do, even if you're not asked to do it. Nobody can phone up to complain, because they don't know who to complain to; branch managers have disappeared. The trouble with all that is that the new hi-tech culture is diametrically opposed to the old high-touch culture. With IT, banks can get rid of people, get rid of paper, get rid of property and not necessarily notice that while they are doing all this they are getting rid of relationships with customers at the same time. And that, give or take a bit over a couple of decades, is what happened in banking in Britain and in many European countries.

And customers? Well, they were just taken for granted. While the advertising hype was sustained, customers found it increasingly difficult to deal with the bank. The branch may have been closed and a centralized enquiry system installed. When customers called to ask for information they were shuffled from one department to another, hanging on to the phone while wallpaper music dribbled into their ears. Customers became, in the language of so many so-called service companies, Revenue Earning Units. This is a telling and dismissive phrase. It characterizes a contemptuous attitude to customers and almost deliberately encourages uncaring and thoughtless behaviour amongst staff.

The impact of all this on retail customers was appalling. When there was no personal relationship, nobody to talk to, no single individual to deal with, trust between the bank and its customers turned to dust.

Then came the banks' next self-inflicted blow. When there was a recession, when banks were having a bad time with bad debts, largely created by their own misjudgment, they attempted to recover by getting really tough with small customers, many of whom had been with them for generations. Branch managers' views on their local customers' long-term creditworthiness were largely ignored as the banks destroyed hundreds of small businesses in their own panic to stay alive. So the relationships that had been so painstakingly built up over generations, already fairly shaky, were completely destroyed. In current consumer surveys in most European countries, brands of fizzy drinks, running shoes and jeans inspire much more trust than banks.

Why did banks get themselves into such a hole? First, because in the clash of cultures between technology and marketing, technology was seen to bring vast economies and people only vast expense. Second, because in their rush for profit banks became greedy and careless. They charged for everything they could think of, often without telling their customers, and they started making mistakes in administration. And third, banks stopped valuing the branch manager system. Top management thought it was old-fashioned and expensive. They didn't realize that what they were busy undermining was a highly sophisticated, flexible structure for service marketing in which the bank culture was underlined and emphasized. They didn't even realize that the branch manager system had anything to do with marketing. Marketing, they thought, was something to do with large advertising budgets and changing the signs and colours on the fascias of their branches. Silly them! In other words, banks brought all the disasters on their own heads through greed and short-sightedness.

So now what are they going to do? Most large financial service institutions realize that their relationships with customers are bad; most want to rebuild these relationships, preferably without too dramatic an increase in their overheads. Many are recreating a system around relationship management, which means that each customer has at least in theory one person inside the bank with whom he or she can create a long-term partnership – the branch manager, under another name. The relationship manager refers them to a specialist when there is a particular need. Some banks are thinking of going further than this. They have noticed that clever marketers like Disney and Nike have been reinforcing their retail presence and they are beginning to realize that they have a massive, underutilized asset in their prime locations. They are looking at turning redundant branches into social centres, Internet cafés, information areas – all with banking and other financial service facilities attached. They are beginning to appreciate that if people walk into their store just to browse, they may buy. They're also having to work hard at training their staff to be nice to people. They may even put relationship managers into these branches. So for a few banks the wheel is turning full circle. Well, they don't have that far to look!

There are always a few organizations that resist the conventional wisdom and do what they think works best. Svenska Handelsbanken never, even in the headiest days of on-line banking, the Internet, centralization and all that, gave up focusing on its branch network. According to the *Financial Times* in an interview with Lars Grönstedt CEO, '30 years of consistent focus on its branch network is behind the bank's growing market share and its ability to present a return on equity above the average of its Nordic peers for each of the past 29 years. "Continuity is something that banking customers appreciate more than we generally realize," Mr Grönstedt says.'[1]

The *FT* article continues, '… the Handelsbanken model is not simply about having more branches; rather it is the striking degree of autonomy the branches are given that sets the bank apart… Branch managers can choose their customers and the product mix they wish to work with… Handelsbanken's model of branch independence "is unique because of the extent to which the principle is applied. All customers, private and corporate, whatever their size, are the responsibility of a local branch."' Even very large corporate customers like, say, Volvo are managed locally. But of course the branch buys in specialists from the centre. In other words relationship management, which is now being painfully discovered for the first time by most banks, was there all the time. According to the *FT* article this system puts Handelsbanken at the top of the efficiency league among European universal banks. Credit losses are lower, staff are more fulfilled, customers are happier and a virtuous circle develops.

Can such a model work outside Scandinavia, the article asks? Well, in my observation most people regardless of their country of origin prefer good service to rotten service, so what's the problem? In Britain where in 2001 Handelsbanken had just started operations, Mr Grönstedt says he has noticed how customers have responded to small details such as the staff giving direct telephone numbers. 'That single little detail seems to make a great impression when you talk to new customers. England seems to have been "call centrified".' Throughout all the dramatic changes Handelsbanken seems to have been able to hang on to a real, genuine, 'old fashioned', but now of course very modern service-based culture.

For most banks, though, bringing the service element back into their business is now profoundly counter-cultural. Since the mid-1970s banks have been taught that their entire future depends on their mastery of technology. It's a bit hard to strike some kind of a cultural balance between hi-tech and high-touch when you've thrown high-touch out on its ear, even when you can see that hi-tech by itself isn't working. Now, as they move into new areas of distribution, financial service businesses, acutely aware of how they have undermined their own brands, are introducing new and, as they hope, more effective brands: Egg and Smile in the UK, Solo in Finland, Banque Directe in France, ComDirect in Germany, Patagon in Spain, Japan Net Bank and so on.

The dreadful experience that retail banks have had in service branding should be a lesson for others who want to go down the service route. Hi-tech does not replace high-touch. It complements it. When you utilize a lot of hi-tech, there is even more need to reinforce high-touch. This means training all your people to understand that they represent the brand, that they actually *are* the brand as far as customers are concerned. It means that you, the company, should not depersonalize the customer into a Revenue Earning Unit.

Those are the issues that make service branding big and complex. It happens that traditional marketing orthodoxy has not really begun to tackle or even properly to comprehend them. In so far as all this is beginning to emerge it's presented in terms of what marketing people are now beginning to call 'internal marketing'. What they mean by this is spending some time and effort on marketing the product/service they are dealing with to staff. But this misses the point.

Another anecdote. A team of us were doing a study for a Portuguese bank. One of my colleagues visited a branch in a small town in northern Portugal. The branch manager was waiting for her – all primed. She asked him what was the most important factor that governed the branch's attitude. 'Service,' the branch manager said. 'Marketing. Really giving the customer warm, personal, accurate service.' There was a pause. Then he said, 'There's only one problem.' 'What's that?' my colleague asked. 'Well, you see,' the branch manager said, 'As you know we close for lunch between 12.30 and 4 pm. And do you know that's exactly when most of the customers want to come. How can we give them service when we're closed?' Needless to say the branch manager had just come back from a marketing course.

The best service brands take real pride in what they provide. They get satisfaction from pleasing customers who aren't treated as Revenue Earning Units, but as real people. Look at the Four Seasons Hotel Group. On the whole, staff like working at Four Seasons hotels because guests notice how good the service is.

All this has very little to do with conventional consumer product marketing. It means that most of the traditional marketing orthodoxies and traditional marketing suppliers are an irrelevance. Advertising agencies can't help. There's no money in advertising to internal audiences and anyway they don't know anything about it. Direct mail and the rest of the promotional activities so dear to the conventional marketer's trade aren't much use either. It's a hearts and minds job.

Companies can learn from soccer teams, elite military units and similar organizations, where people need to depend on each other to build an unbeatable team. In the future the model for brand management in a service business may be the British Army's Special Air Service, an elite unit built around mutual support, or the Brazilian soccer squad, rather than Fairy Liquid dishwashing detergent. Managing a service brand must not be a discrete and separate activity that is isolated from the rest of the organization. It draws its strength from being a central part of the whole business. Svenska Handelsbanken works well because its entire system of operations is built around a service culture.

Of course lots of new consultants have set themselves up to deal with internal communications, and once the charlatans and the peddlers of psycho babble have been pushed to one side some of these new suppliers will prove to be valuable. But you can't succeed just with good consultants.

The heart of the problem is that almost all companies are organized into separate departments with rigid lines of demarcation, which bear no relationship to the way in which things actually work in real life. A Revenue Earning Unit only exists inside the empty and mindless world of the planning department in a corporate head office. In real life you can only achieve service effectiveness through interdepartmental co-operation and through looking at the business as a whole, the way a customer does. Corporate structures don't take account of this. Just as in school, history and geography are really one subject, because a nation's history is profoundly influenced by its physical location, so in companies, marketing and sales, credit management and recruitment and training are all intimately and inextricably interrelated. Have you noticed the difference between what happens when you buy a policy from an insurance company and what happens when you make a claim? The language, the style of behaviour, the speed of response are all completely different. When you buy, you're Mr Nice Guy. When you claim, you're a suspect fiddler. This is because there is virtually no training inside most insurance businesses about what they really stand for – about real corporate standards and attitudes. There's a lot of jargon and platitudinous waffle, but nothing serious. And it's also because there is no conversation or discussion between different parts of the organization. The department looking after credit risk and fraud learns nothing about the history, personality and integrity of the customer from the people who sold the policy in the first place. You won't get your people to live the brand unless they work together as an entity in mutual dependence. You simply can't manage it with a series of vertical divisions; you can only manage it by joining them together.

The easiest way to look at this is to examine how a brand inter-relates with its audiences. My former colleague Michael Wolff calls this 'the journey'. In a well run, thoughtful, service-driven organization, as far as staff are concerned the journey starts with the process of recruitment – the recruitment advertising, the website, the letters, phone calls, e-mails, interviews – then it moves through induction, training, working on the job, learning with a mentor and learning on courses with peer groups, to consistent and regular appraisals from colleagues. Gradually, both through explicit and implicit training, through absorbing what has been taught, observing the behaviour of peers and bosses, and through experiencing the way the company or brand lives in its own environment, a true sense of what the brand genuinely stands for will emerge.

If a company wants to do all this properly and thoughtfully, it means big organizational changes. The entire budgeting process has to be re-evaluated, with intangibles given a higher priority. Co-operation between human resources and marketing people has to become as close as the traditional relationship between marketing and sales. Recruitment activities, induction and training programmes all have to embrace the service concept. Suppliers and partners of every kind have to be indoctrinated in the ethos of the brand and the organization behind it. Environments have to be designed which enable staff to see that the company means what it says. Then there is staff communications, which doesn't mean talking a lot about not very much, but being relevant, honest and honourable. There's where people sit and how they work together. This affects issues of open plan or closed offices. There's timekeeping, dress code, everything that affects the way people live and work within the organization. Every detail matters, because detail is what people notice and live by. You can't eat, drink or sit on vision and value statements.

It's partly a question of making connections that at first sight seem unlikely. Organizationally it implies the development of some kind of matrix between the conventional divisions and the processes which involve journeys through the brand of staff, of customers, of suppliers and partners.

That's why even the most unlikely areas of corporate activity have to be examined to see where and how they can help in reinforcing the appropriate behavioural patterns. Food, for example. What quality of food for whom? What choice? What price? Where do you eat it? Is the place called a restaurant or canteen? Is it single status or are there different restaurants and for that matter different choices of food for the various grades of staff? Or, to put it another way, does the organization demonstrate hierarchy in the food it serves and the way it serves it?

In the truly behaviourally driven organization one of the most important activities will be customer service – more accurately called complaints. Analyzing what went wrong very carefully, putting it right very fast and learning the lessons so that it doesn't go wrong again are perhaps the most important factors in creating an environment in which service brands continually improve. Complaints or customer services should be a central and high-profile activity in any service organization. It should be consistently and actively monitored by marketing people, because it's the bit of the organization that actually tells you how you are doing. Right now, it's the part that nobody likes to deal with. It's messy, unpleasant and apparently unrewarding. Some companies, more than you might think, don't even bother to reply to complaints. Ryanair, the cheap and cheerless low cost nil service airline, has such a reputation. And almost all companies if they're honest will admit to fobbing people off. Everyone knows that the happiest customer is the one whose complaint was properly dealt with. So why don't we do it? Because we don't care enough and we can't really be bothered. Because somewhere or other the customer is only a Revenue Earning Unit.

And it all starts, as it always does, at the top. This whole process has to be driven by the chairman or CEO, through a small but powerful steering group of appropriate brand minders. You don't expect a business like Ryanair to deal with complaints. For what Ryanair charges you can't expect great service. But a high-price carrier should be different. If the chairman of Iberia can't be bothered to get one of his people to investigate a potentially serious complaint, and to sign a polite letter to his customer apologizing, how does he expect the rest of the organization to behave?

Some national cultures have managed service a lot better than others. In Singapore and in Japan, levels of service in my personal, anecdotal experience, are of a much higher general standard than in the US or Europe. It's also probably the case that service brands in the US are a bit better than those in Europe. And it may well be the case that the UK is bottom of the table, as my Asian, European and American colleagues insist. But nowhere is that good at it.

There are in the end a very few simple rules for sustaining service brands. They are:

- Organize your operation around the brand. Get all the different bits – sales, service, complaints and accounts – to talk to each other and to understand what the brand stands for so your people can truly give service and so they truly want to.

- Train your people to live the brand.

- Behave the way you talk.

- Always remember your staff are the brand.

- Be consistent and coherent.

- Treat customers with respect. Remember they are not Revenue Earning Units but the people who can make or break your company.

- Listen to customers by putting service or complaints (or whatever you like to call them) right in the heart of the brand, where you can respond.

- Lead by example from the top.

And once you've done all this, trust your people to live the brand.

BRANDS ON A GLOBAL STAGE
HOMOGENEITY, HETEROGENEITY AND ATTITUDE

For all the major businesses that are developing
into single corporate global brands there are an almost
equal number that are doing exactly the opposite.

CHAPTER 5

Stand by a construction site practically anywhere in the world and you'll see huge yellow machines crawling on their tracks looking like something out of a science fiction movie. They are scraping, digging, smoothing and moving dirt, rubble and rocks. These are Caterpillar machines in their element, on their home ground. Wherever there's a building site anywhere in the world, it's home for Caterpillar. Caterpillar of Peoria, Illinois, USA, has been making construction equipment since about 1890. The company is called Caterpillar because some of its equipment moves on caterpillar tracks, like a tank. In fact the first tank designers in 1915 got the idea of tracks from Holt-Caterpillar tractors, one of Caterpillar's predecessors.

Caterpillar has a turnover of about $20 billion. It is one of the US's leading exporters. Caterpillar is a Fortune 100 company. It has plants in 42 countries and many subsidiaries, some of which, like Perkins Diesel, are major global brands in their own right. Although it is active in a lot of industries, its roots are in agricultural machinery and its reputation is based around construction and mining equipment. Caterpillar's position as the world's leading construction equipment builder has been frequently challenged, most recently by Komatsu of Japan, but it remains the greatest name in its field.

'Most Americans associate Caterpillar Inc. with heavy machinery,' says an article in the *Wall Street Journal*[1], 'but in Europe, the brand is now a fashion statement. After backpackers and sport utility vehicles, international urbanites have latched onto "Cat" gear as the new symbol of American outdoor culture, with an air of durability and honest hard work.'

Cat got into merchandising round about 1990, but the business didn't properly take off until about 1994. In 2001 Cat merchandise – that is, 'apparel, accessories and giftware' – accounted for $1 billion, which is, say, 5% of turnover. You can also buy Cat Racing products and 'over 300 styles of boots, shoes and sandals for men, women and children'. 'This merchandise,' says Cat on its website, 'reflects the rugged, reliable and durable quality of the best earth-moving equipment in the world – Caterpillar machines and engines.' I'll say it does.

Cat seems to have got into work clothes initially to boost its image with people who use its equipment all over the world, but the casual clothing business is moving in and a lot of its new European customers would never knowingly go near Caterpillar equipment. Many young men and some women too are of course interested in looking and acting tough, and by some strange kind of osmosis Cat equals Tough, so the Caterpillar brand now appears on tough-looking clothes and boots. Like Cat equipment, Cat clothing is now a global brand. It projects more or less the same values everywhere in the world.

In branding terms this is, of course, called line or brand extension. In one respect there's nothing new about it; it's been going on for years.

But Caterpillar brand extension is a bit different. It's perfectly rational to assume that if you make confectionery you can move into ice cream, or that if you can make toilet soap you can make shampoo using the same brand name. But bulldozers and boots? Anybody who thinks about it for even a moment will realize that the kind of expertise needed to design, make, sell and service construction equipment is a million miles away from the world of clothing – even tough clothing. But in the hugely emotional world of branding, nobody thinks like that – certainly not the young men and women who wrap themselves in yellow and black windcheaters bearing large Cat logos on the back. What is happening is much more than product extension. It's attitude extension – quite different and much more interesting and significant. It's one of the next big steps in global branding.

Caterpillar brand extension doesn't have much to do with the products that the company makes; it's to do with the attributes that the Cat brand is seen to possess worldwide. It's about attitude. Caterpillar is about Tough – so Tough is Tough machines, and by extension Tough clothes, Tough boots and anything else Tough that you care to think of. Tough camping equipment – tents, sleeping bags, stoves and all that – would work. So would Cat tennis racquets and ski equipment, and while we're about it what about a range of Cat cafés serving blood-red meat and strong lager, or a Tough energy drink that competes with Coke and Gatorade – Catade.

Caterpillar's roots lie deep in Mid-West US agricultural country, along with John Deere, McCormick and the other great (and once great) companies of America's farming belt. Caterpillar was and no doubt still is an engineering company with a deeply ingrained product-based mindset. Does it have any real idea of the true potential value of its intangible assets, and does it have a culture in which these can flourish?

Cat coyly doesn't tell us what proportion of its profitability comes from merchandise, so we don't know how important Tough clothes are compared with Tough machinery in the current balance sheet – probably relatively little – but we can pretty well guarantee that from an external awareness point of view, merchandise is coming up fast. Cat merchandise must have huge psychological significance outside the company. How much it has inside the company is an entirely different matter.

Suppose Caterpillar finds over time that its competitive position is beginning to erode? Plenty of Caterpillar's peers, Mid-West equipment companies with their roots in farm equipment, have gone under. If Cat finds that it can't make a living out of its traditional businesses, because people in other parts of the globe are making products just as good only cheaper, wouldn't the company be wise to focus on a property that nobody can imitate, nobody can beat on price, nobody can take away, that is unique to Cat – the Cat brand? My guess is that Cat would have to be near death's door before it accepted that thesis. According to Angela Wilkinson, Head of Special Projects at Shell, the reason why engineers reject the emotional content of what they create is because the thought of a product having a personality or life of its own drives their own insecurities about losing control. For a technocrat she says, 'Emotion equals loss of control.' Perhaps

that's why changing a technically based culture to a marketing-
(or seduction)-based culture is very hard.

When a brand has a clear attitude, what can and increasingly
does happen is that attitude complements or sometimes even
replaces the product as the core idea behind the global business.
This hasn't happened to Caterpillar and maybe it never will but
Cat does have astonishing opportunities. Caterpillar is already
the Tough brand globally, just as Nike is the Winning brand.

If Cat is mostly product, and attitude has emerged partly at
least through opportunity and good fortune, Virgin is exactly
the opposite. Virgin is practically all attitude. What distinguishes
Virgin's businesses from their competitors in any field is not
what they do, but the way that they do it. With Virgin, attitude
issues are more central than Caterpillar's because Richard
Branson's businesses have always been about attitude – *his*
attitude. From its very earliest days, Virgin has been a personality
business and Richard Branson has never been shy of presenting
himself and his businesses as defenders of the little man against
the corporate baddies.

Virgin's products and services are not selected on the basis of any
special product knowledge or competence that exists inside the
Virgin business. They are selected on the basis of opportunity. If it
seems there's a market for it, the deal is OK, the timing's right and
there's a partner with product knowledge, Virgin will go for it.
The assumption is that if Virgin goes into trains or financial
services or cell phones or anything else, it can buy in the expertise
from outside; it can outsource. Virgin Trains is part owned with
Stagecoach; Virgin Financial Services is linked to the Royal Bank
of Scotland; Singapore Airlines has a large chunk of Virgin Atlantic
Airlines, and so on. Whatever the business is – vodka or condoms –
it will be done in the Virgin way, with the Virgin attitude.

Virgin describes itself as a 'branded venture capitalist which
contributes the brand, cash and expertise to its 200 companies'.[2]
Well, that's one way of looking at it. I'm not sure that many

venture capital or for that matter private equity businesses would necessarily agree – in fact I'm pretty sure they wouldn't, because they only bring financial and business expertise (sometimes) to the party. They make no claim to having branding expertise. Venture capital or private equity businesses don't create families. They sell on. They're not like Virgin at all, where one brand dominates everything it does.

Now the conventional wisdom, the orthodoxy, is that if you have one very powerful brand globally, with more or less one name, one visual identity and all that goes with it, and you get one bit of that business wrong, it will have an adverse effect on every other part of the business, and the whole will suffer. Well, strangely that doesn't seem to have happened to Virgin. Parts of the business have been just terrible, like the trains. Perhaps fortunately for Virgin, Virgin Trains are located only in one country, the UK, where Branson's personal reputation is strongest. But media comment on Virgin Trains in the UK has been disparaging almost to the point of libel. Interestingly, though, other parts of the Virgin empire, the better bits, don't seem to have been much affected by the plastering that the bad bits receive. Does all this mean that the brand is more important than the product? Well, strangely perhaps in this case it seems to be. If the London to Scotland West Coast rail service is unreliable, dirty and expensive, you would think that calling it Virgin makes it even worse because it betrays brand values. But somehow or other, despite this disaster, Virgin as a whole seems to have sustained goodwill. Is this because of Richard Branson's personal associations with the brand? Is it because of his quasi-heroic status, intrepid balloonist, slayer of the fat cats, informal, young (well, not old anyway), doer of good deeds? Probably. Richard Branson cultivates a high popular profile. For many people, I suspect, hard-playing, hard-driving, fun-loving Branson is Virgin – and whatever its and his faults they like him and they like his attitude. Strange but true, it seems that Virgin is deemed innocent even when it is proved guilty.

Virgin, with all its faults and weaknesses, appears to be a prototype of a particular kind of global business – one in which everything that can be outsourced is[3]. The corporation finances (sometimes), designs, brands and markets the products or services. Everything else, including manufacture, is carried out by specialist third parties. In this model, which is likely to emerge side by side with more traditional patterns, the brand must inevitably emerge as the most significant differentiating factor for the corporation.

This kind of brand not only attracts certain types of customers who will, because of the brand's characteristics and attitudes, follow it as it moves from one business sector to another, but it also, and crucially, attracts high-quality suppliers, partners and staff. It is the brand's attitude and behaviour, supported and sustained by its visual manifestations, that are its prime assets. In the case of Caterpillar the possibility of such a development exists; Virgin, a much smaller and altogether more fragile but more brand sensitive enterprise, is already making it happen.

Many very large companies are tentatively moving in this direction, but only the very far-sighted seem to be able to break out of the conventions that traditionally bind them. In the oil industry, as in so many others, the last decade of the twentieth century saw massive reshaping through mergers and takeovers. The result of all this was (as I write, it's still going on) Chevron Texaco, Exxon Mobil, Total and BP. The first three companies are more or less the same as they were before the mergers happened, only a lot bigger. BP, however, is quite different. When BP took over Amoco the name change to BP Amoco lasted about five minutes. While BP was digesting Amoco for lunch it took over Arco. Then early in 2002 it bought Aral, Germany's largest petrol retailer. BP Amoco Arco never happened at all – it was back to BP again … while the Aral brand seems at least for the time being to be staying. Why did all this happen? Because BP, formerly British Petroleum, formerly Anglo Iranian, formerly Anglo Persian, originally created as a national supplier of oil to the Royal Navy, became under John Browne's leadership, Beyond Petroleum, a tree-hugging, environmentally friendly energy business striving very hard to be unlike any other. The phrase 'Beyond Petroleum' appears to have stretched credibility too far

BP's former, rather military looking logo.

The new face of BP – all warm and sunny.

and it seems to have been quietly dropped. BP, like most oil companies, has a history which by today's standards of political correctness does not bear very close scrutiny. Now, though, it wants to be a major player in the drive to create sustainable environments, and for an oil company that's attitude and a half. BP simply can't manage to create and sustain credibility unless it is seen to be changing dramatically.

BP is not only talking about sustainable environments, it's pouring huge amounts of money into dealing with these issues. It has an agreement with Cambridge University, Imperial College, Princeton, University of California at Berkeley, the California Institute of Technology and the Chinese Academy of Science on 'strategic and technical issues relating to the development of cleaner sources of energy' and that's just for starters. Its advertising, its new symbol, its newly redesigned petrol stations, its vast research and educational programmes, and its massive corporate sponsorship programmes in the arts are symptomatic of the effort BP is making to reposition itself as the global energy company that cares. This is just part of BP's overall development. The company is so determined to focus only on what it does best that it's moving into outsourcing in a big way. It's even outsourcing people management. In many ways BP is beginning to look like one sort of twenty-first century global enterprise with a twenty-first century attitude.

It's easy to be cynical and suggest that this is simply an attempt to climb on to the environmental bandwagon, or to cloak activities in places like Colombia in which BP appears to have behaved in traditionally insensitive oil company fashion, but the overall effect of BP's new attitude is to make it look rather different from many of its competitors. Would potential recruits want to work for a respected company – or a pariah? Would governments want to deal with an organization that has a record for protecting the environment or with some of its competitors who patently don't care? In a world in which environmental issues are beginning really to matter, and where corporate behaviour and misbehaviour is coming under the closest possible scrutiny, BP's new unalloyed global attitude, whether introduced out of enlightened self-interest or altruism, seems pretty smart.

HSBC also wants to be seen as a global player but is a bit more ambivalent about the whole business. The quaintly named Hong Kong and Shanghai Banking Corporation, now calling itself HSBC, has grown from its roots financing Scottish opium traders in the Far East in the buccaneering period of Victorian imperialism, through canny acquisitions and extremely efficient management, into one of the largest financial service institutions in the world. HSBC has taken the view that if it wants to be a global bank, in the same league as Citibank, it had better have a global brand. So with one or two relatively minor but important exceptions, it has changed or is changing the names of all its acquisitions worldwide to HSBC. Some of the banks it has bought, like The British Bank of the Middle East, Marine Midland in the US, Midland in the UK, Banco Roberts in Argentina, Banco Bamerindus do Brasil in Brazil, CCF in France, and its Canadian and Australian operations, were amongst the best known banking names in their local worlds, but HSBC has had the will, the courage and the ambition to dump their names in favour of its own profoundly unmemorable and somewhat misleading name. Many of my acquaintances around the world are convinced that HSBC is Chinese, and are amazed to learn that its origins and culture are lowland Scottish. In fact the choice of HSBC as a global name for the bank seems almost perverse. In addition to a bank with global ambitions inappropriately implying that it is Chinese in its origins and funding, the name is also confusing. HSBC, British but with a distinctly Chinese accent, is competing with BSCH (Banco Santander Central Hispano of Spain). What were they thinking of? Well, if you can get away with HSBC as a global name, you can get away with anything.

HSBC has an admirable boldness of ambition but it's linked to an extraordinary clumsiness of execution. The name HSBC is bad enough but the truth is that the company does have a strong, attractive and unusual attitude, which for some strange reason it has neglected. Its values are in reality clear, powerful and idiosyncratic. Keep a low profile. Actions speak louder than words. Keep your mouth shut and let the world judge you on your performance and so on. All stuff straight from the Scottish manse. Fine traditional thinking and the right way to set a young ambitious Scotsman landing in the British crown colony of Hong Kong in the 1920s on the right path. Suitably adapted for today's circumstances it would work well but the company has ignored these in favour of a much blander approach.

According to its website, HSBC's values are:

- The highest personal standards of integrity at all levels

- Commitment to truth and fair dealing

- Hands-on management at all levels

- Openly esteemed commitment to quality and competence

- A minimum of bureaucracy

- Fast decisions and implementation

- Putting the Group's interests ahead of the individual's

- The appropriate delegation of authority with accountability

- Fair and objective employer

- A merit approach to recruitment/selection/promotion

- A commitment to complying with the spirit and letter of all laws and regulations wherever we conduct our business

- The promotion of good environmental practice and sustainable development and commitment to the welfare and development of each local community.

Well, you'd hardly expect a bank to say it had no integrity, that it was committed to fraud and dishonest practice, and to bureaucracy, and so on. In other words the values statement is full of the usual platitudinous although unexceptionable stuff, and one hopes that HSBC performs effectively on even half of it. Citibank or Deutsche Bank or Bank of Tokyo might well say exactly the same kind of things – and probably do. HSBC somewhere or other still seems to be loyal to its lowland Scottish, austere, canny, thrifty roots. HSBC doesn't like stars. But if HSBC's fundamental attitude is 'judge us on the way we behave', then it should say so, quite unequivocally and consistently. As I write, HSBC is running an advertising campaign based around the idea that it has intimate local knowledge. Global but local, so to speak. We seem to have heard something like that before. It's not original, it's not particular. And above all it has nothing to do with the bank's traditional values. It's all a bit of a mess. Dear dear.

Interestingly, and perhaps significantly, one of the very few brand names that HSBC has retained is First Direct, the telephone and Internet bank brand originally started by Midland Bank (now HSBC) in the UK. First Direct was aimed at self-confident, youngish, successful people – back in the '80s they were called 'yuppies' – who were not intimidated by banks, who understood a bit about finance, who wanted to manage their own affairs and feel that they were in charge.

First Direct was largely about communication and behaviour. The name, the clear black and white visual style and the very powerful simple, confident images communicated the bank's attitude in advertising. But it was attitude that drove the brand. From the very beginning staff behaviour was exemplary. First Direct has become one of the most admired financial service brands in the UK. It has real personality and it really seems to believe in service, and that's presumably why it is one of the very few brands that HSBC has had the good sense to keep.

For companies that recruit and train people and market products globally, the conventional wisdom is that it makes sense to operate, if they can, under one brand name which represents one clear idea everywhere. It helps in the development of a single corporate culture that staff can embrace regardless of their own nationality, religion and ethnic origins. It makes recruitment easier: potential candidates have some kind of idea of the corporate reputation. It makes promotion of products and services easier and cheaper: new products or activities can be introduced on the back of those that already exist. Everyone who deals with the organization, from suppliers to partners to local and central governments to customers, will have a more or less clear idea about the business, and that makes the whole process of managing it much easier. This is particularly true if the brand which represents the business has a clear attitude, like Virgin or BP, or even if the attitude emerges by accident, like Caterpillar. It's much easier to move into a new market with a well known brand than with a proliferation of brands. It's more economical because it costs less in organization, recruitment, marketing and virtually every other activity. It maximizes impact and enables the brand to take advantage of global, cultural or sporting events like the Olympics or the World Cup. And that's why corporations believe in global brands.

But of course all this has a powerful homogenizing effect. Taken to its logical conclusion it makes everything look, feel and act the same everywhere. And of course the homogenizing impact of the global brand is another stick the anti-branding lobby brandishes. But, more important, customers have noticed this, too; a single global brand may have varied emotional values in different places, which is why homogeneity is being challenged by an equally powerful branding principle which exploits heterogeneity, proliferation and diversity.

As usual, when you start examining brands in detail, you find that global branding is not quite so powerful after all. For all the major businesses that are developing into single corporate global brands, there are an almost equal number that are doing exactly the opposite.

In real life many people don't want what their neighbours have. Lots of people don't want to be inclusive; they want to be exclusive. What this means is that in the twenty-first century, regardless of what the companies that own brands want, heterogeneity will be as influential as homogeneity in global branding developments. And in certain areas of business it is and will continue to be much more influential. Look at this from Krug[4]:

Krug: Established in 1843, Krug has specialized in producing solely prestige and exceptional champagnes. With Krug dedication to quality takes precedence over quantity of production.

Krug is the only Champagne House still fermenting all of its champagne the old way: in small oak casks – necessary for developing Krug's intense bouquet and complex flavours. Since there is no precise formula for Krug Champagne, the memory of the original Krug taste has been passed on intact from generation to generation in the Krug family. Today both 5th and 6th generations supervise directly every phase of production, tasting and blending Krug.

In this piece of promotion material, as in everything else it does, Krug is underlining its independence. But as it happens Krug isn't independent at all. It is one of fifty-plus brands comprising the portfolio of LVMH, Louis Vuitton Moët & Hennessy, which claims to be the largest luxury goods producer in the world. In 2001 LVMH had a turnover of $13.26 billion and it employed 56,000 people around the world. LVMH collects brands with attitude.

LVMH has five business groups. The first group is wines and spirits, including Moët & Chandon (once described to me by a French friend as the Renault of champagne), Château d'Yquem (perhaps the Lexus of wines, or have I got that wrong?), Hennessy, Hine, Krug and a lot of others. The second group is fashion and leather goods, including Marc Jacobs (American), Loewe (Spanish), Kenzo (Japanese), Givenchy (French) and Thomas Pink (English). The third group is perfumes and cosmetics: this is mainly but not exclusively French – Givenchy, Guerlain and Dior plus others. The fourth group is watches and jewelry, including TAG Heuer, and the fifth is selective retailing, including Le Bon Marché and La Samaritaine. These brands come and go. The ones that perform well are kept; others are thrown out and replaced. It's quite likely that by the time you read this the company's portfolio will be a bit different.

Although LVMH is massive, its brands go to enormous lengths to sustain their own individual pedigrees. Each is seen to be completely independent and self-sufficient. The lengths to which this philosophy is taken is pretty impressive. In the town of Cognac in France, Hennessy's home, there is a Hennessy exhibition centre which is a kind of shrine. Hennessy bottles, books, memorabilia, even if I recall correctly a Hennessy boat cruising up and down the river. And you don't even smell the faintest whiff of LVMH.

LVMH brands like Hennessy are at the top end of their respective sectors. All of them trade on very powerful personalities and attitude – quality, design, exclusivity, apparent independence and everything that goes with it. The LVMH mission statement which says 'our products and the cultural values they embody blend tradition and innovation and kindle dream and fantasy' has got it just about right.

The peculiar and particularly fascinating thing about LVMH brands is that, although they have no overt associations with the business as a whole, they all seem genuinely driven by its values – creativity and innovation, product excellence, image, entrepreneurship and striving for the best.

Most of the brands, like Hennessy or Krug, derive from businesses that have a long and admired tradition and history of their own. LVMH appears to have resisted the temptation to undermine the brands and reduce them simply to shells. Their integrity, individuality and attitude – at least looked at from the outside – remain. No potential customer would know that Hennessy French cognac, Louis Vuitton French bags and luggage, Kenzo Japanese high-fashion clothes or Loewe Spanish leather goods have anything to do with each other. Each presents itself as completely independent, and many, like Vuitton and Loewe, overlap and actually compete. Presumably, where it is possible, in the back office, in financial management, information technology, human resource management, purchasing, distribution and so on, group resources operate, but the customers don't come across any of that.

The group as a whole is synonymous with Bernard Arnault, whose aggressive not to say ruthless behaviour towards peers and competitors is legendary. Shareholders may not know all the brands, but they are certainly familiar with the company's attitude, while customers associate themselves completely with individual brands and for the most part have no interest in or knowledge of the business as a whole or the parentage of the brands they buy. For them the brands are independent entities. But this also means that LVMH is not a corporate brand and it doesn't have the concomitant strength, power and coherence of one brand. It can't promote itself as a whole publicly on a global stage; it can't present a public corporation and attitude. Insofar as there is a corporate presence or personality, it is manifested in Bernard Arnault himself.

Having a portfolio of powerful brands is a huge strength because it gives LVMH several bites of the cherry in each of its chosen sectors, but it is also, inevitably, extremely costly. While on the one hand it means that the individual values of each brand can be sustained, even maybe enhanced, it also means that each brand has to have its own promotional budget, distribution system, sales staff and so on. Furthermore it's unlikely that any single brand would be able to dominate its sector, simply because with fifty-plus brands even a very large enterprise can't give each of them as much promotional budget as most of them must want.

LVMH is only one of a number of major global companies that own and manage a portfolio of brands. Diageo, which owns Guinness, Johnnie Walker, Baileys, Gordon's and many other brands, is in a similar situation; so is Prada which, apart from its famous Italian brands, owns amongst others German fashion house Jil Sander and English shoe company Church's. Interbrew, the almost anonymous Belgian beer business, also owns a number of brands, like Beck's, which to all outward appearances thrive on their independence.

Multi-brand businesses are not just confined to luxury goods and food and drink. Media businesses like AOL Time Warner,

Bertelsmann and Rupert Murdoch's News Corporation are also based around a complex mix of brands. Many of Murdoch's businesses like *The Times*, *Sunday Times* and the *Sun* newspapers are confined only to a single country; others, however, like the publishing house HarperCollins have global reach.

Communications groups like Omnicom and WPP are particularly fascinating because their subsidiaries, major advertising agencies, PR companies and branding consultancies, advise the world's large corporations on global brand strategy. I've read lots of portentous and much sensible stuff about global branding strategy from various companies inside these organizations. And yet their own brand strategy is, to put it kindly, hard to figure out. Physician, heal thyself. These major companies have their roots in advertising agencies. WPP, which were the initials of a small, rundown, quoted company called Wire and Paper Products operating at the less glamorous end of the promotions business, was the vehicle that Martin Sorrell used to build up one of the biggest communications groups in the world. Brands like J. Walter Thompson, Ogilvy & Mather, Young & Rubicam, Landor, Hill and Knowlton, just to pick a very few, are nurtured by Sorrell in much the same way that Arnault looks after LVMH brands. In Sorrell's view apparently it wouldn't be commercially desirable, or for that matter feasible, for all these businesses to merge (although there do seem to be rather a lot of them, and perhaps a bit of judicious pruning wouldn't go amiss) because they would lose their magic and they would also lose their customers. Each company or brand has its own specialism. Also, a bit like traditional fmcg companies, it would seem that the more brands you put on the shelf the better the chance of being picked. Or in this case the more of your own companies you have on a pitch list the more chance you have of winning the job. Unlike LVMH brands WPP's businesses don't even share one single attitude. They aren't all passionate about creativity; some are, some aren't. In fact apart from Sorrell's own formidable drive, obsessions and personality, it's difficult to know quite what does hold WPP together. Financially driven perhaps? So maybe WPP isn't a communications group; perhaps it's a financial holding company.

In its own idiosyncratic way *Vogue* is a global brand. UK, Spanish, Russian and Japanese *Vogue* have sister editions in nine other countries.

VOGUE

MARCH
£3.20

THE
BODY
WE ALL
WANT
NOW

GET
THE
NEW
LOOK

FASHION
AND
POLITICS
HOW TO
DRESS FOR
POWER

international
collections issue

VOGUE
ESPAÑA

EXCLUSIVA
CAMERON DIAZ
Y LEONARDO
DICAPRIO
**ATRACCIÓN
SALVAJE**

**LAS
NUEVAS
REGLAS
DE LA MODA**

Primavera '03: las
tendencias que funcionan

MODA &
PASIÓN
LENCERÍA DE COLOR
MICRO-MINI
ESTILO ROSA
SILUETA SEXY

QUÉ
SALVAR DEL
INVIERNO
LAS PRENDAS
QUE SIGUEN
TRIUNFANDO
EN VERANO

SÓLO
PARA DOS
SPA EN PAREJA
VIAJE A MALDIVAS
SALIR DE NOCHE

VOGUE
NIPPON

3
March
2003
No.43
¥780

ヴォーグ ニッポン

ミニスカ大論争。
春にときめく
バッグ&シューズ。
浜崎あゆみ、
秘密のクローゼット。
輝く！新世代・セレブ。

ファッションもビューティも、
キーワードは
フレッシュ・グラマラス！

**Catch
a wave**

この春、史上最強のサーファーガール。

絵とバッグの
トランプCARDS

VOGUE
РОССИЯ

НОВЫЙ СЕЗОН
ЦВЕТ САКУРЫ
АТЛАСНЫЕ ПЛАТЬЯ
ПЫШНЫЕ НАЧЕСЫ

РУССКАЯ МОДА
30 ЛУЧШИХ
КОЛЛЕКЦИЙ

КРАСОТА
ОТ ПРИРОДЫ
ПРОЗРАЧНЫЙ
МАКИЯЖ
ПАСТЕЛЬНЫЕ
ТОНА

АББА
НАВСЕГДА
30 ЛЕТ
ЛЕГЕНДЕ

**ВЕСНЕ
ДОРОГУ**

It's rather difficult for many of these global brand-owning businesses to handle the issue of attitude. Some of them, like LVMH or News Corporation, have a large personality deriving from the individual who runs them. He is the business as far as the commercial and financial world is concerned: Arnault is LVMH, Murdoch is News Corporation, Sorrell is WPP. Others, like Diageo, have tried to develop a corporate attitude separate from the brands they own. When Diageo sells itself to recruits or potential partners or financial journalists, it claims that what holds the businesses together is that through its brands the group markets everyday pleasures, small but enjoyable relaxations, to people, everywhere in the world. Diageo, like LVMH, is obsessive about building its brands and where possible extending them. Others, like AOL Time Warner, seem to be so busy attempting to hold their various businesses together that they don't bother.

Once upon a time Ford only had one brand – Ford. Then it acquired Lincoln. Now look at it. Ford Motor Company, through its Premier Automotive Group, manages Volvo, Jaguar, Land Rover and Aston Martin brands. It also has a chunk of Mazda. Under the skin most of these brands share some features, but as far as customers are concerned they are different – different shapes, different sounds, different smells, different prices, different dealers. Each of these brands has been modulated for different sectors of the market place. Each of these brands has an attitude which suits certain types of customer. Ford's Premier Automotive Group operates through these brands because it believes that its customers want choice and exclusivity.

This is the branding philosophy that rules at LVMH, Diageo, Omnicom, Prada, VW, DaimlerChrysler, Bertelsmann, News Corporation, WPP and of course at Nestlé, Unilever, Danone, Procter & Gamble and many other companies.

At the heart of it lies a paradox between the requirement both for homogeneity and heterogeneity, between a single, mighty, overwhelming global brand with a clear attitude and the consumer's need to pick 'n' mix between brands to create an identity that suits him or herself.

And if a substantial part of the attitude is rarity, specialization, particular knowledge and exclusivity, then homogeneity simply doesn't work. In other words it's the nature of the sector in which they operate that drives homogeneity or heterogeneity in global branding. And it's always a difficult call. To assume, as so many people do, that branding leads to homogeneity is simplistic and naïve.

There are other factors too that influence the way in which corporations organize and therefore present themselves. Some of these factors, which will have a huge influence on corporate life and behaviour, I examine in the next chapter.

WHY BRANDS ARE IMPORTANT INSIDE COMPANIES

BONDING AS MUCH AS BRANDING

As companies mutate into global coalitions with fluid management structures, shifting borders, alliances and business activities, brands increasingly emerge as the most significant spiritual and cultural glue.

CHAPTER 6

PREVIOUS PAGES
The office as mall.
The interior of British
Airways' head office at
Hounslow in England.

Most companies who built brands in the early days were anonymous entities lurking about in the business pages of newspapers. Although their brands were well known to the consuming public, the companies behind the brands tended to keep themselves in the shadows. Their annual reports were miracles of opacity in which as little as possible was revealed. Their executives rarely gave interviews to the press, and when they did they stuck firmly to a business agenda. There were no personal revelations. They were command and control organizations, usually based in one or at most two countries, which often exported their products around the world. The bulk of their employees, mostly blue collar workers, came from one country, often even one town. Although some of these companies were not very nice to work in, quite a few were. Many went to very great lengths to create and sustain a loyal and contented workforce. They didn't project their brands internally but they did try to create loyalty to the corporation as a whole. They were paternalistic; some were philanthropic. The best of these organizations tried to create a corporate family. Some even put up villages for their workers – Krupp in Essen in the German Ruhr, Titus Salt at Saltaire near Bradford in Yorkshire, Cadbury at Bournville, Birmingham in the English Midlands, Lever at Port Sunlight, Liverpool, Hershey in Pennsylvania, Philips in Eindhoven, Holland – and turned their workforce and their families into real communities. But everybody knew his place (and it usually was 'his') and there was a strong sense of belonging. As late as the 1960s at the Cadbury factory there was a bicycle shed by a rustic gatehouse which, if I remember correctly, bore the legend 'For Directors' Bicycles Only': the quintessence of hierarchical modesty. It was usual in these kinds of companies to have orders of precedence and status that were quite military. There were several levels of canteen, carefully graded according to rank and size. The position of an executive's office, its size, colour scheme and quality of rug or carpet were all carefully specified. Personal relationships between ranks were usually formal, 'Mr X' and 'Sir' or their equivalent. This kind of bureaucracy was stultifying and drear, but it certainly bred cohesive relationships, shared language, mores and behaviour patterns – a strong sense of corporate identity, in fact.

There are still companies like that around although they are gradually dying. But an increasing number of organizations are emerging, some even from the embers of traditional entities, that are quite different, and they live side by side with more traditionally structured companies. These companies are formed from a complex web of alliances and joint ventures with research, design, manufacturing and marketing activities all over the world. They operate from a small headquarters. They employ or work with highly educated people from a mix of different countries; certainly not blue collar workers, or even white collar workers – more like T-shirt workers (the management guru Peter Drucker calls them 'knowledge workers') whose primary loyalty is to the technology they work in. The idea that these companies should provide housing or in any other way participate or, as some people might prefer to put it, interfere in the domestic lives of their co-workers is utterly alien to them.

Companies like this are often so complex, so amorphous, so flexible or all of these that they aren't easy for an outsider or even an insider to understand. They are also very difficult to hold together because there is very little emotional glue inside them. No sports events or formal activities like outings; just informal and frequent evenings at the bar – and of course the inevitable away days.

The old vertically integrated companies were all about hierarchy, rules, and command and control from the top. Although that structure had great weaknesses – rigidity, local focus, promotion by seniority, narrow outlook and so on – it also had huge strengths. A well structured system like an army or a police service can engender the most remarkable loyalty. Gold watches for forty years of service were not a joke even though we may jeer at them today. They were a real tangible award for dedicated service.

The new businesses are not like that. Not only has the structure of the corporation changed but the workers have changed too. In the old days there was cohesion on the shop floor. Drinks with the lads. Life in the same street. Marches with the Trade Union led by shop stewards and a brass band. But work and loyalty patterns and skills have changed completely. In these new organizations, where there are relatively few unskilled people, where much of the discipline is self-imposed, where hierarchies are loosely defined, where boundaries are fuzzy, employees themselves reflect the corporate culture. They don't want to be patronized, or as they might put it 'nannied'; they're not very interested in collective bargaining by trade unions on their behalf. And the last thing they want is a paternalistic employer. Many no longer expect or want a long-term relationship with the organization they work for.

Not only is the kind of work we do different but the way people are treated is different. There is no longer much real job security. Jobs for life with a guaranteed pension at the end are increasingly being replaced by careers based around job skills and knowledge. IT experts live in their own world where there is much more focus on technical skills and opportunities than on the company in which these skills are to be applied. If an organization doesn't suit them, people leave and go somewhere where they can get on better professionally. Companies hire and fire more promiscuously. Increasingly people work on a freelance or part-time basis, some from home, or a long distance from corporate headquarters, sometimes in a completely different country; maybe in call centres located in Calcutta dealing with customers in California or Clydeside. All this means that loyalty to the corporation is harder to create and sustain.

The whole world of business is different. Chief executives come and go as fast as some employees, and companies grow and shrink at the most alarming speed. The Internet sector is not the only manifestation of such volatility. In 2001, fourteen of the Fortune 100 companies had not been in the list more than five years. Once-huge corporations regularly bite the dust. In the US, of Pan Am, Bethlehem Steel and Chrysler, just to take three great names of the 1960s, one has disappeared completely, the second is bankrupt and the third is now controlled by a German company. Incidentally, as my colleague Jesus Encinar points out, Pan Am appears as the logo on the space vehicle in Kubrick's epic movie *2001: A Space Odyssey* made in 1968. For Kubrick Pan Am was an icon of American permanence. He could imagine all kinds of major changes, but he couldn't imagine that Pan Am might not be around in 2001.

There's an external dimension too. When times are good everyone wants to work for the employer with the best reputation, where the pay is reasonable, working conditions are pleasant, colleagues are friendly and the company does a job that everybody, including the employee, can be proud of. The financial community wants to invest in companies that are patently successful. In other words the reputation of the corporation and its brands, the admiration or respect they engender, the trust they create, has a direct effect on recruitment, relationships with partners, the financial world and the wider communities in which the organization lives.

As companies mutate into global coalitions with fluid management structures, shifting borders, alliances and business activities, brands increasingly emerge as the most significant spiritual and emotional glue holding organizations together and representing their reputation to all the worlds with which they deal. Brands become the prime manifestation of the corporate purpose. That is why they are important not just for customers, but for the people who work for or deal with the organization as employees, partners or investors. In a changing, turbulent world where everything else is opaque the brand's status as a symbol for the company and what it makes and sells becomes central. Apart from having an internal, focusing, stabilizing role, the brand is an outward symbol of continuity, clarity and coherence. In some organizations the brand and the corporation are of course synonymous.

Airbus is one of these new, volatile, fluid entities with permeable borders and no clear shape. Airbus's roots go back to the 1960s when the squabbling aircraft companies of four European nations began reluctantly to realize that, unless they co-operated with each other, the much larger American aircraft industry would destroy their own commercial aircraft industries. There had of course been plenty of joint ventures between European aerospace companies before. Concorde was an example of Anglo-French collaboration (or lack of it); VFW Fokker was a rather low-key failure between Dutch and German companies, and there were many others. Led by the French, a design and construction alliance called Airbus was formed from French, German, British and Spanish aerospace companies to build civil aircraft in competition with the Americans. Meanwhile in the US Boeing had defeated its rivals Lockheed and McDonnell Douglas in the civil market, so that left only Airbus and Boeing in the big league. By now the one thing that kept the Airbus consortium together was that its partners hated and feared Boeing more than each other – just. Like all other major corporations Airbus is stuffed full of Mission, Vision and Values Statements. Its real Mission, though, is and always has been simple, clear and short: 'Get Boeing.' That's why it was formed and that's why it exists. Over the years Airbus grew to design and build a wide range of commercial aircraft which directly competed with its hated rival. Airbus is now a highly successful organization, at least in terms of market share, with what one can reasonably assume to be a good long-term future. Although its headquarters are in Toulouse and the French element dominates, the Germans are equal shareholders and also have a significant position. Design and manufacture take place all over the world, although the principal suppliers are mainly European. In the first decade of the twenty-first century Airbus, after an extended period of pain, turmoil, plots, counterplots and betrayals worthy of Grand Opera, is becoming a genuine company.

The British design and build the aircraft wings and various other partners are responsible for other bits. BAe Systems is only a 20% partner in Airbus because of vacillations of various British governments long past and is therefore not quite as significant as the French or the Germans in the mix. However, Airbus is largely a subsidiary of another company – the European Aeronautic Defence and Space Company (EADS) – which began as an alliance of the Franco-German-Spanish aerospace business. EADS has no British shareholding. And to further complicate matters, BAe Systems has very close relationships with some American competitors of EADS (and therefore of Airbus). All this makes the Airbus business a quite typical big commercial enterprise of the first quarter of the twenty-first century. It is global, it is full of alliances, the knowledge content is big and the metal-bashing element is small, leading to higher added value, and many of the people who work on Airbus don't work for it, they are contractors or subcontractors. It is therefore quite difficult to know where Airbus begins and ends, who is a partner, who is a competitor and what makes the whole enterprise work.

Within EADS, the largest shareholder in Airbus, there are, apart from Airbus itself, a multiplicity of alliances, joint ventures and projects; in some of these competitors co-operate, in others partners compete. Umpteen companies from many nations are involved. EADS as an organization has no clear borders. All that really matters are the projects. It's a bit like building houses in London in the eighteenth century, or for that matter making a movie today: for every project a new, individual and slightly different team is assembled. It's almost impossible, unless you are an expert in the field, to follow who is co-operating with whom on which project. All this makes life complicated for anyone who deals with the organization. Airbus is complex, and EADS even more so.

It's pretty difficult for the workforce of both organizations too. A worker in a BAe Systems plant in Filton near Bristol, working on Airbus wings, is employed by BAe Systems. BAe Systems is a partner in Airbus. So who does the worker think he's working for, BAe Systems or Airbus? To which organization should his loyalty be directed? Airbus is one of the two leading civil aircraft constructors in the world, but Airbus is a long way away from his own world. It's difficult to explain to him precisely where he fits in and how. What does he have in common with a colleague working for EADS in Hamburg? So although the Bristol and the Hamburg workers are both working for Airbus, one works for BAe Systems and the other for EADS, who are, wait for it, competitors. The two men don't eat together, read the same newspapers, watch the same TV, or see each other often. Even if they did it probably wouldn't help much because they might not share a common language. So not much bonding there.

But this situation is fairly simple compared with an IT subcontractor for Casa, the Spanish partner both in Airbus and in EADS, many of whose people will probably be on short-term contracts and work on a freelance basis from home. Some of their work for Casa may even be for a competitor of EADS or Airbus. Who do they think they work for? What pride can they take in the final products? Team loyalties, bonding, shorthand, understanding each other, mutual reliance remain as significant today as they have ever been, and the new companies that are emerging, including Airbus, are pretty short on all of these, even though in many respects Airbus and its partners try very hard. But partly because of the way they are organized and partly because of the spirit of the age in which we live, there is a lot of misunderstanding and waste that in more cohesive units can be avoided. It's a problem. And it can be an overwhelming one.

Sometimes alliances don't work because they are undermined from within. Large enterprises which never seem quite large enough on their own do deals with erstwhile rivals to take on the world. Concert was a joint venture between AT&T and BT aimed at handling the tele and info communications issues of global companies. AT&T and BT were so keen to make Concert work that according to newspaper reports they didn't even write provisions for a divorce into the marriage contract. But that didn't help when the project failed. It just made it harder to separate. The problem with Concert was first, that it didn't attract customers; second, that both of its parents were competing with it; and third, that internally within Concert the partners just didn't get on. There were too many culture clashes between them. There just wasn't enough to hold it together.

Despite all this, these new kinds of businesses formed from alliances are popping up all over the place. In airlines, a business long hindered by the crassest kind of nationally based protectionism, there are at last clear signs that a competitive environment is imminent; in fact in certain parts of the market it has arrived with a bang, and this is, of course, leading directly to alliances. oneworld, led by American Airlines and British Airways and including the dreaded Iberia, and Star Alliance, led by Lufthansa and badly wounded but still breathing United Airlines and involving Thai, SAS and Varig, BMI and a bunch of other national airlines, are typical examples of the new consortia that are beginning to emerge. These alliances and joint ventures embrace national airlines that are traditional competitors and have very strong individual identities and cultures based around the countries from which they derive. So what do the Star Alliance partners have in common, apart from the fact that they are commercial airlines using the same aircraft – more or less? Not much. The participating airlines in these alliances all claim remarkable benefits. Staff are all trained at least publicly to welcome the alliances. Quite what they really make of their mutating organizations is difficult to judge. Customers seem rather confused by it. Speaking from a sample of one, I don't like finding myself on American Airlines (uncomfortable) when I thought I had booked on BA (comfortable) and I hate the idea of being forced to fly Iberia. In other words, the standards of service, size of seats and everything else a passenger notices vary so much from one airline to another that for the moment these so-called alliances are, from a passenger point of view, simply booking systems designed to suit the airlines. It's true that passengers are bribed into loyalty with lots of frequent flyer Air Miles. Otherwise, though, the alliances appear as yet to bring virtually no customer benefits. Things will only change when the alliances really gel and some new, genuine entities emerge. And that of course will mean dropping national names, identities and affiliations, and creating new identities and new images that everyone who deals with them can respond to – brands or, if you prefer, corporate identities. The reality here is that because branding has hardly begun, nobody, staff or customers, can make much sense of what's going on.

Like airlines, steelmakers have always been high-profile national flag carriers. Traditionally they employed large numbers of people in capital-intensive plants. Steel mills were managed on military lines with clear borders, hierarchies, and command and control structures. In the first half of the twentieth century images of the steelworker dominated industry. In Stalin's Soviet Union,

Stakhanovites were awarded national heroes' medals for prodigious efforts in steel mills or coal mines. In the 1930s and '40s serious-minded corporate films showed stokers shovelling coke into the furnaces of steelworks. The imagery of the Machine Age was personified in the pale-faced, wiry industrial worker with oil or coal dust streaked all over his face, making his small, personal but vital contribution to national prosperity and wealth. The steel worker had a short and arduous working life, but he was proud of his craft, at ease with his mates and in a certain way admired by the community. Krupp was not the only steel company that housed and cherished its workforce. In Soviet Russia the company town with company schools, company hospitals and company stores was the norm. Tisco, Tata's steel company in Jamshedpur, Bihar, India's most corrupt and lawless state, was one of the most remarkable examples of paternalism at its best I've ever seen. Jamshedpur was a beacon of cleanliness, light and integrity in a sea of dirt, darkness and corruption.

Now national steel producers are struggling to survive. The US steel industry is in terminal decline despite desperate attempts to save it with tariffs. In Europe old national steelmakers are huddling together to survive. The Dutch and British industries have combined in Corus. The greatest names have gone and a few new players have emerged apparently from nowhere to recreate the industry in an entirely new way. Lakshmi Mittal, an Indian educated in Calcutta, living in London with a business quoted on the Amsterdam and New York stock exchanges, runs a company called LNM. Part of the group, for reasons which are obscure (to me, at least), is called Ispat ('steel' in Sanskrit). Ispat has steelmaking operations in Mexico, Trinidad, Canada, the US and elsewhere. In addition the group controls steel mills in Indonesia and Kazakhstan. As I write, the organization is negotiating to take over the collapsing and monumentally inefficient Romanian steel industry. In 2003 LNM became the second largest steel business in the world and it claims much the most profitable. The success of the business is based around technology, an eye for opportunities and a complete lack of concern about national market places: 'Emerged, emerging or submerging markets: they all represent

The Star Alliance brand gradually emerges (above) and then dominates each individual partner (below).

opportunity to me,' Lakshmi Mittal is quoted as saying[1]. Above all there is a determination to manage in a different way from the old dying steel businesses. Who could have conceived of a successful global steel business based around mini-mills, a new type of process for scrap, with operations in the most unlikely places? In Ispat there is no interest in glorifying or bemedalling the workers, giving them subsidized housing, free education and health services, or creating national icons. It's a capital-intensive, technologically driven, unsentimental, global business which, so far at least, shows not the slightest signs of philanthropy, paternalism or even concern for its various workforces. If it is to work effectively in the longer term it will have to develop a new culture. In an organization where plants are located all over the world and where executives and workers have widely differing backgrounds in religion, language and most habits and customs, it's mandatory in the longer term for the organization who employs them to develop a culture which they can all share and relate to. Just how this curious mix of operating units will mutate towards this is another story and one that Mittal does not yet seem to have started on. But for LNM these are relatively early entrepreneurial days so we'll have to wait and see.

Glorifying the industrial worker. A Soviet poster from the Stalin period.

Aerospace, airlines and steel are relatively easy for any of us to comprehend. Life sciences businesses are a lot harder. Amersham is a classic example of the new life sciences world. Its major constituent parts come from Northern Europe, Britain, Sweden, Norway and the US but it has absorbed or formed alliances with complementary organizations in many other parts of the world, including Japan. Amersham is one of the *Financial Times*'s top 100 companies and in 2003 employed 9,500 people, of whom 5,000 are graduates and 1,400 are PhDs. Its businesses, which are to do with imaging and biotech, don't have as much in common as you might think, although they are beginning to converge.

Each of the principal constituents of Amersham has been an important company in its own field and each has had a remarkable history. Amersham itself started off during the Second World War as a UK government laboratory for the extraction of radium.

It went on to become the very first business the Thatcher government privatized in 1982. Nycomed, a pharmaceutical company, was started in Oslo in 1874 and became one of Norway's most high-profile and successful companies. In 1985 it was named Norway's 'Company of the Year'. Pharmacia, a major Swedish pharmaceutical company, developed an early lead in the biotech field both through its own research and through a clever acquisitions policy. In 2002, after a merger with US Upjohn in the 1990s, Pharmacia fell into the open jaws of Pfizer and ceased to exist.

Amersham, the corporate brand, and its two divisions – all clearly related to each other.

In 1997 Amersham International (as it then was) merged its Life Sciences division with what had become Pharmacia and Upjohn's Pharmacia Biotech in a joint venture called Amersham Pharmacia Biotech. Shortly afterwards Amersham International merged with Nycomed to form Nycomed Amersham. The strategy was to take a 'leading position in molecular medicine – helping to provide predictive diagnostic and screening products along with gene based therapies, tailored to the individual patient's genetic profile'. So the company doubled and then nearly tripled in size – quite suddenly.

Naturally this created indigestion. The propensity for an organization like this to operate in separate units entirely or at least in units largely independent of each other was almost overwhelming. The organization employed thousands of brilliant scientists in several different locations; it had a number of very different, highly regarded national traditions of achievement, of which three were dominant; it had half a dozen different national backgrounds and a wide range of clients located globally, few of whom were overlapping. And the whole enterprise had come together at lightning speed. Unless some structure was created that would engender loyalty to the group as a whole, there was always a danger that centrifugal forces would undermine the success of the entire business. If a highly volatile, very clever, opportunistic organization is going to grow very fast, its constituent elements have to work together, have to respect each other and have to be seen to be co-operating and moving towards one single goal. Hence the Amersham branding programme, which was aimed not so much at customers as at

Amersham

Amersham
Health

Amersham
Biosciences

the internal world of the company and the external financial and scientific communities from whom it had to earn respect and understanding. You can call this branding – but it's a very different kind of branding from the sort that's involved in launching a new ice cream, and it hasn't got much to do with traditional marketing management. And it's the kind of thing that Airbus, the airline consortia such as Star Alliance and Ispat will all have to put in place – sooner rather than later, if they are going to be effective rather than dysfunctional in the medium and longer term.

In a very thorough, well organized, comprehensive programme led by the Chief Executive and the Corporate Head of Communications, and using every conceivable form of media, in 2001 Nycomed Amersham relaunched the corporate brand. The name was shortened from Nycomed Amersham to Amersham. Its two businesses were simplified into Amersham Biosciences and Amersham Health. A new visual identity was introduced that showed that there was one group consisting of two businesses which were separate from but related to each other and to the whole, and a clear story explaining the role of the business and its constituents was communicated.

In presentations all round the group at all levels, on every site in every country, the advantages were spelled out. Success in any part would benefit the whole. Marketing spend would have more impact. Explaining the group and its structure would be easier. The potential to innovate scientifically and technologically would be increased. And so on. All these were real and palpable gains. Great stress was laid on the collective corporate heritage. The traditions and background of each company in the group were underlined so that everyone from everywhere felt part of the family. But the fundamental idea was to generate staff loyalty to the entire business and get the external financial and scientific communities to understand the businesses, what they did and how they worked.

It was not a conventional marketing operation aimed at customers. It was really a 'hearts and minds' internally focused programme. Bonding as much as branding. And in an organization that depends almost entirely on finding and keeping research brains, that is critical. Amersham management celebrated the launch of the new identity with an award of 1,000 share options for every single employee on the payroll, a latter-day equivalent of traditional corporate benevolence.

It seems to have worked. Outsiders, financial analysts and others do seem to understand what the company is about and internally the various constituent parts of the group are pulling together in a way that was inconceivable before the programme was launched.

Is this a model for the new kind of business? Probably. These businesses, Airbus, Ispat and Amersham, although they are so very different in terms of activity, size and structure, share certain characteristics – a mix of nationalities, high levels of expertise, global attitudes, plants and market places, and an extremely varied group of companies from which the enterprise has been formed. What's different is the way each has (or has not) handled the branding issue, and that in turn relates to their priorities and also their immediate focus.

Each of these companies exemplifies the changing nature of the corporation and its mutation from a rigid, national, highly structured, vertically integrated, formal enterprise into a loose, confederated system, almost a partnership, with unclear boundaries. This new type of corporation is so unstructured that it needs to create and sustain the corporate sense of purpose and reputation so that people of all kinds will choose to work with it. Amersham has recognized this and is dealing with it. The others are at various levels of enthusiasm and comprehension in their attitudes and behaviour.

All these businesses and others like them have been profoundly influenced by the three major issues – globalization, technology and deregulation. But there's another factor that influences most of them. It's where their boundaries lie. In a sense you can call it brand extension but it's much bigger than that; it's perhaps more like business extension or activity extension. It's about what they can or cannot cope with within a single business and brand framework. If your name is powerful enough, what can you do with it and where can you take it? El Corte Ingles and Carrefour or Wal-Mart can sell groceries and clothing and financial services. What's to stop them issuing credit cards? Nothing. They do. The power of the brand is so strong, the faith it creates is so real, that we just assume that if Carrefour or Wal-Mart or Aldi or Tesco is behind it, whatever it is, it will be OK. Tesco, according to Merrill Lynch[2], has very big ideas for the 'portability' of its brand. It has 'its eyes on telecommunications, utilities, ticketing, travel and leisure'.

But these are relatively simple examples of brand stretch compared with what is happening in some parts of corporate life. In some businesses the apparent potential is so vast that it's very difficult for businesses to know where their appropriate boundaries lie. El Corte Ingles sells cars but could it brand them too? Is El Corte Ingles a retailer or could it appear to be a manufacturer? Dixons has a house brand. It's called Matsui, which pretends to be Japanese. Dixons doesn't put its own name on its products, because it takes the view that a Japanese-sounding name has greater credibility.

Some kinds of businesses have such vast potential and are so amorphous that putting up boundaries is genuinely very difficult. Look at telecoms, for instance. Until the 1980s the world's telephone businesses were boring old state monopolies. Then their whole world was turned upside down. Deutsche Telekom or France Telecom or Spain's Telefónica are still traditional fixed link phone operators, but they have also moved in very different directions. They went through phases of rapid geographic expansion, technological expansion into WAP and then out again, voice and data, cell phones, broadband; everything. They were in entertainment and then out of it and some of the time they didn't seem sure where they were. Some telecoms businesses went into consultancy as well as entertainment. Syntegra, a BT company, competes directly with EDS and Accenture in the systems consulting sector, a world which could not be more different from entertainment. Is it really credible that one business can span everything from consulting to entertainment? In these kinds of businesses even the brand isn't strong enough to hold the business together. No wonder some of the world's largest infocoms companies make so many mistakes. No wonder they seem to change their minds so quickly. No wonder that at least some of the time they don't seem to know what they're doing. They are just dazzled by the power that the combination of their financial resources, their brand image and the opportunities available to them offer. Peer group pressure draws them into doing things they don't properly understand, with partners they don't really know, in places they are entirely unfamiliar with. Telecoms is not particularly unusual. It's just an extreme example of a familiar pattern.

In the 1980s there was a fashion for automotive and aircraft businesses to come together. BAe bought Rover, Daimler Benz (as it then was) had DASA, and Saab Automotive and Aerospace were part of one concern. Within a decade that fashion had disappeared and not one of those companies any longer has joint automobile and aerospace links.

In situations as turbulent and tumultuous as these, where businesses are going global, outsourcing so much that they become a shell, getting flatter management, employing people on contract, using more part-timers, forming flexible alliances and joint ventures both with friends and traditional enemies, either crystallizing these into new companies or breaking them up and starting again, moving into business activities which appear at first sight to be quite remote from their traditional worlds; in this kind of climate what do people of all kinds, wherever they come from and whatever their relationship with the company, have to hang on to?

Only reputation. Only trust. There is nothing else. And how do you encapsulate and project trust and reputation? Through the brand name and the brand values – what we used to call corporate values and corporate identity. And that, paradoxically, is why brands are perhaps more important to corporations in their internal, domestic, working lives in today's turbulent and tumultuous times than they have ever been before.

'**MADE IN...**' WHAT DOES IT
MEAN AND WHAT IS IT WORTH?

The nation and the brands associated with it are deeply entrenched in the collective psyche...but the national brand with a few exceptions is in terminal decline.

CHAPTER 7

Baileys Original Irish Cream, you may be shocked to learn, did not originate in Ireland; nor was its creator a Mr Bailey. Its moving spirit, if you'll forgive the word, was Tom Jago, a new product development expert, a Cornishman, who together with his colleagues David Gluckman and Hugh Seymour Davies devised the concoction 'while we were trying out cocktails with the knowledgeable barman at the Dorset Hotel in mid-town Manhattan'[1]. The name came to the trio in a bistro below Gluckman's SoHo office. Naturally it was researched. In focus groups Baileys received a 'unanimous negative response. They hated the stuff and didn't believe it was Irish or even real. We suppressed the results.' I like that. Tom Jago is evidently a man who really understands the value of focus groups.

As everyone knows, Baileys went on to be a great success. It is one of the world's Top Twenty spirit brands, and has been blatantly imitated and plagiarized at least half a dozen times. So why is Baileys so astonishingly popular? It has been marketed with great skill and flair and with huge budgets. Its distribution is superb. It is ubiquitous. Whether you're in London, Nairobi, Shanghai or Mexico City, you can't escape from it. It's not only a drink, it pops up in coffee, in chocolates, and in almost every other form you can think of. You can't yet take it intravenously, but they're probably working on it. It's even possible that part of its appeal lies in its taste – although some people might find that hard to believe. The packaging must help. The deep browns, greens and golds seem redolent of an authentic, ancient Celtic past. And this is surely it. To my mind what makes Baileys so special is its apparent Irishness. Like virtually all alcoholic drinks, Baileys is perceived to have strong, deep and traditional national roots.

Nationality fuels alcoholic drinks. Virtually all wines, beers and spirits proclaim their country of origin as an integral part of their branding: Czech lager, English ale and Irish stout. Indian beer, like Kingfisher and Cobra, is brewed partially at least for consumption with Indian food in Indian restaurants all over the world. Tsingtao, descendant of a brewery established in German Chinese Concession territory, is the beer of choice with Chinese

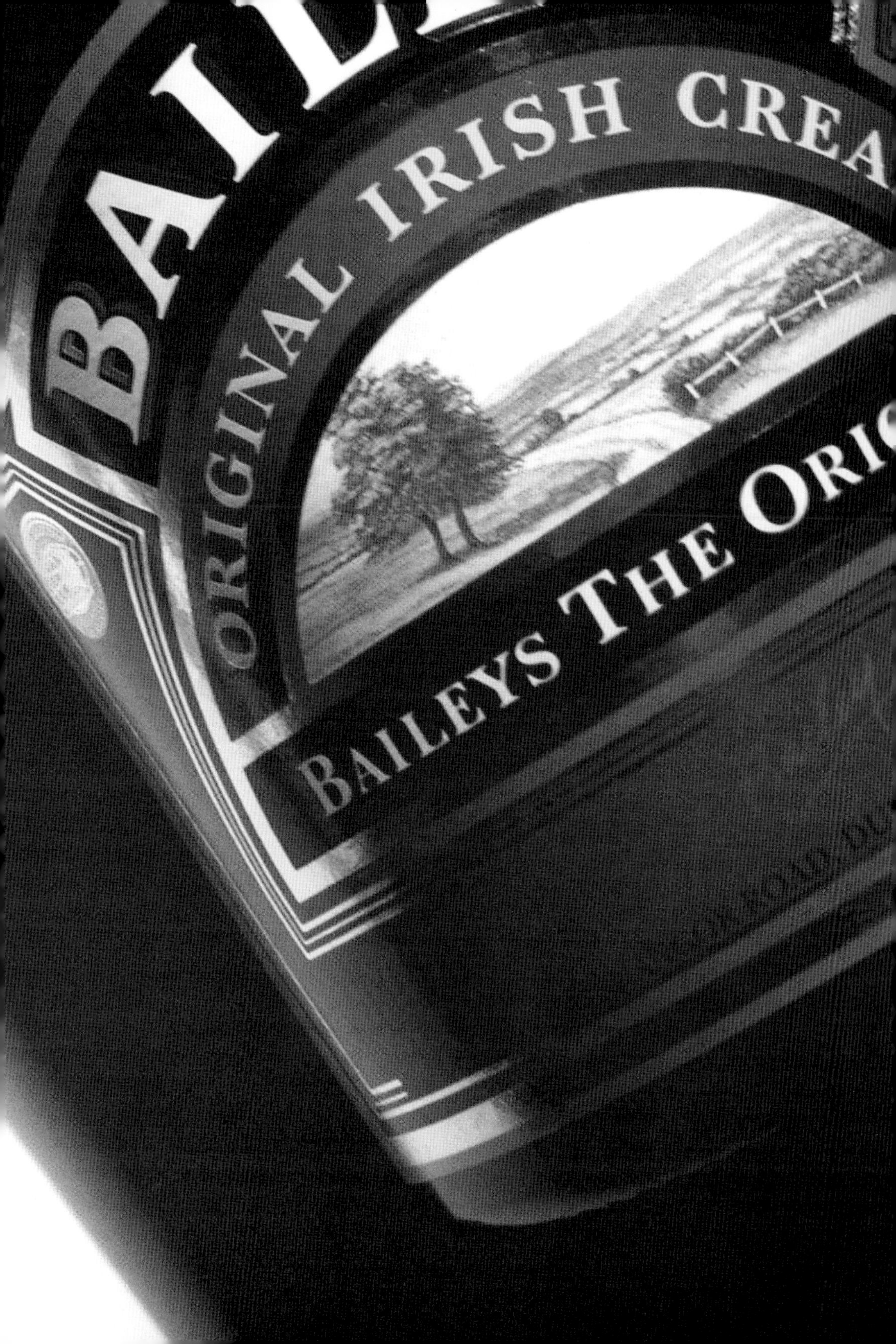
ORIGINAL IRISH
BAILEYS THE

food. Kronenbourg comes from Alsace, so it's a kind of Franco-German mix; Carlsberg and Tuborg are Danish; Heineken is Dutch; and Sol is Mexican. Budvar from the Czech Republic squabbled for years with Bud from the US over who owns the name Budweiser but their taste and brand personalities are very different; there isn't any doubt about which product comes from where.

A similar formula applies in wines. French, Spanish, Italian wines are all categorized by region and grape. In addition there is the quality and nature of the terrain and the idiosyncrasies of the growers to consider. In France the categorization of wines is particularly complex, sophisticated and subtle. Wines from each region have markedly different characteristics. Bordeaux wines are quite unlike those from Burgundy: the grapes are different, the soil is different, even the shape of the bottles is different, and there are variations even within these two regions, each with enough subtleties to keep oenophiles gainfully employed on a permanent basis. In Germany until relatively recently wine labelling was so arcane that you needed a handbook to find your way around it. The opportunities this afforded for showing off were endless. Each region had different bottles. Hock bottles are brown. Mosel bottles are green. Wine from Franconia comes in a special stubby-shaped bottle called a *bocksbeutel*. All this is very important commercially. These complexities say 'this is the real thing'. No imitations. That's why French champagne producers who come from the area around Rheims called Champagne have defended their collective description so vigorously against producers of sparkling wines from other French regions and more particularly from other countries. New World wines from Australia, Chile, New Zealand, South Africa, the US and so on follow the same complex patterns although usually with rather less intricacy. So the end result of all this is that the nation itself is seen to be the font from which wine flows. That's why the idea of Eurowine, wine from a cocktail of countries, seems absurd, even repellent.

The same issues apply with whisky. Scotch whisky is said to derive its particular characteristics from the natural qualities of local

Beer brands almost always emphasize their national origins. These are from (left to right) Japan, Czech Republic, India (but brewed in the UK), Italy, Singapore and China.

water and soil and from the inherited genius of those who distill it. Single malts come from different areas and each has its own special flavour. Irish whiskey (with an e) is different from Scotch, and Bourbon is different again. However clever Suntory the Japanese whisky distillers are, they can't make whisky like they do in Scotland.

What all this boils down to is that in many kinds of food and drink, especially drink, nationality is some kind of seal of quality. Nobody in their right mind would buy Italian whisky or for that matter Scottish olive oil.

We all take for granted without really even thinking much about it that in the world of alcoholic drinks the nation and the brand are inextricably intertwined, but this is only the most overt manifestation of a relationship that has been around since goods were first traded, that is still very much alive, and that is being very rapidly undermined.

In the nineteenth century most countries made products primarily for their own domestic consumption although for some nations some kinds of exports were very important. Almost every manufactured product varied greatly by country. French, German, American and British railway engines were different from each other even though they all operated on the same gauge. Each major nation had its own steelworks, munitions factories, chemical and soap plants, shipyards and so on, with individual idiosyncrasies. Everything from bread and cakes to architectural styles and modes of dress had a national flavour, and they were often very important.

Competition was intense. In the Franco-Prussian War of 1870–71, the German-made needle gun was superior to its French equivalent. By the time the new French-designed and built Chassepot came along it was too late – the Germans had won. That's why for the last quarter of the nineteenth century nations aspiring to catch up in military activities, like the Ottoman Empire and Japan, turned to German rather than French advisers and equipment. Naturally there developed an almost symbiotic relationship between certain national flag-carrying products and the nation with which they were associated. When Christian Lautenschlager drove a Mercedes to victory in the 1914 French Grand Prix there was lamentation in France and triumph in Germany. That, together with many earlier and later victories, is how Mercedes came to represent the very best in German engineering and by a process of osmosis the very best in German products. Mercedes became Germany: German engineering brilliance, German technology, German attention to detail, German uncompromising perfectionism. The legend of German engineering prowess grew from the achievements of a few brilliant men in the late nineteenth and early twentieth centuries – Karl Benz, Wilhelm Maybach, the Siemens brothers, Gottlieb Daimler and a few more. They quite unknowingly laid down the basis for the German engineering legend.

Although the reality has changed dramatically the memory lingers on. We were having a conversation about that perpetually enthralling subject, dishwashers, one weekend at my home and a guest said, 'I don't mind what make it is, as long as it's stainless steel and it's German.' For her Germany and engineering integrity were mutually reinforcing concepts. Like most people she didn't know that many dishwashers with German brand names are no longer made in Germany. The halo effect of Mercedes, Siemens and brands like them still continues to give German engineering products credibility. How many people as they sit behind the three-pointed star of their Mercedes M Class SUV are aware that it was made in Tuscaloosa, Alabama?

A similar story applies to Rolls-Royce in Britain. In the Edwardian period it was generally recognized as the Best Car in the World. Eventually it became the best of British anywhere. So Burberry was the Rolls-Royce of raincoats. Savile Row was the Rolls-Royce of tailoring. The Savoy was the Rolls-Royce of hotels. Cazenove were the Rolls-Royce of stockbrokers. Today Rolls-Royce Cars are owned by Germany's BMW (although the aero engine company is still British). BMW are going to the most elaborate lengths to sustain 'Britishness', including building a factory at Goodwood in Sussex where Rolls-Royce cars will be put together – no doubt mainly from German parts. A British site was chosen to add some kind of apparent verisimilitude to the Britishness of the brand. So Rolls-Royce remains a particularly meaningful symbol of British quality – just. The question is of course whether Rolls-Royce Cars is still British or whether, like Baileys, it simply uses nationality as a branding tool.

Sony is as much a symbol of Japan as Mercedes is of Germany. Sony stands for exquisite miniaturization, for technical ingenuity and minimalism. There are a group of Japanese brands that fall into this category – Toyota, Toshiba, National Panasonic, Honda and maybe a few more. But Sony, particularly, seems to embody all of those characteristics of Japanese style that the West so admires. These days, though, many of Sony's products are designed and made outside Japan – and they have been for some years.

In contrast with those companies whose relationship with the nation is symbiotic and mutually beneficial, there are others where the brand is virtually the only idea we have about the nation. Samsung, Hyundai and Daewoo have come to represent Korea but since Korea is still, despite the World Cup, an unknown for most people, these Korean brands are rather empty. If they have any meaning it is that they are simply cheaper versions of Japanese brands which remain for many of us the Real Thing.

Automobiles have always been traditional national icons. They are symbols of speed, independence, status and style, and they are often objects of great beauty, craftsmanship and ingenuity. Above all, at one time they did seem to be the personification of the nation in metal. Just compare and contrast the American Chevrolet, the French Citroën, the Italian Alfa Romeo, the German VW and the British Austin-Healey of, say, the 1960s. All of them were primarily designed and built for their own domestic market place, so they were intended to operate in road and climatic conditions that were quite specific. Each was the national character on wheels.

American cars were built for a country where distances were vast, the climate was extreme, fuel was cheap. Apart from in the cities there wasn't too much traffic and the standard of living was just about the highest in the world. So American cars were very big, cumbersome and frequently ostentatious. They were very quiet, they had air-conditioning and other conveniences, and used up plenty of road space and fuel. That's why American cars, from Chevrolet at one end of the price range to Cadillac at the other, looked the way they did.

The French were getting richer, quite quickly. Their peasant class was shrinking, so the sales of simple rustic vehicles like the Citroën 2CV and the Renault 4 were about at their peak and embourgeoisement was well underway. The Citroën DS was a symbol of everything France was aiming to become – technologically highly sophisticated, very stylish and quite different from anything else around.

For the Italians, whose economic growth rate was also very fast in this period, cars were still romantic, competitive and sporty, and the Italians loved motor racing. Italy has a lot of hilly regions, so Italian cars were designed to corner well and go up hills fast. If they fell to bits after a few years it didn't matter so much; many people could afford to buy the latest model. Because Italians love style, many Italian cars were also very beautiful.

In Germany things were different again. There was a good motorway network with virtually no speed restrictions. This made for tough, well engineered products and discriminating customers. In addition Germany was an economic powerhouse. It was growing richer faster than anywhere else in Europe. Competition between manufacturers was rough and Germany was a serious exporter, which meant that although its cars were built primarily for domestic consumption German makers kept one very big eye open on export markets.

British cars were often technologically quite advanced and the British, despite their unreliable weather, had a lively tradition of small open two-seater sports cars, for example the Triumph TR series, MG and Austin-Healey. Britain made other interesting cars, too, but they were often appallingly badly built. This was a direct result of bad management, terrible labour relations and an out-of-control workforce. Americans called Lucas of Birmingham, who supplied most of the lighting and electrics of British cars at that time, 'Prince of Darkness'. So, like Britain itself in the 1960s and '70s, British cars seemed to have everything going for them, a wide range of products and good design but somehow they always kept failing. Why? Because they were badly made and badly marketed. Moreover Britain was a small country with few motorways where construction faults didn't show up too much. Above all, perhaps, the British motor industry was too pleased with itself and too ready to dismiss competition from Johnny Foreigner. So exports slumped, imports flourished and British products began to wither on the vine even in the domestic market for which they were principally designed.

Japan? Well, in those days Japan just didn't count. Not quite yet.

So the national market still dominated. Manufacturers were so obsessed with designing and building for their own domestic customers, each nation with its own specific idiosyncrasies, that the Ford Motor Company of Detroit had two quite different and competitive ranges of products in Europe – from Ford Cologne for Germany and from Ford Dagenham for Britain. These two ranges of products, both called Ford, competed with each other in dealers' showrooms all over the world. The cars looked different, they had different engines, different technical specifications and different pricing. Apart from the fact that they were both called Ford, they had virtually nothing in common. That was how powerful national brands were. And then Henry Ford II, hereditary chieftain of the Ford Motor Company worldwide, just stopped it.

Ford simply didn't believe his managers when they told him that each domestic market place was different, especially since some European nations were much smaller than many US states. What he could see was duplication of effort, waste on an immense scale, and his managers and executives erecting defensive barriers around themselves so that they could call themselves grown-up automobile manufacturers and not mere assemblers. Under his direct edict therefore Ford of Europe was formed in 1967, with the intention of creating one single range of cars, regardless of which European Ford plant they came from. Most of the experts predicted catastrophe. Around that time I was involved as a consultant both with Renault and Volkswagen. Both companies thought Ford had made a big mistake. But as it transpired it wasn't a mistake at all. Ford had anticipated change. In almost all markets, Ford's market share remained steady. As regulatory barriers fell and the idiosyncrasies of individual market places disappeared, a European market began to emerge and Ford of Europe began to develop a truly European design, manufacturing and marketing policy. Plants in Genk in Belgium, Valencia in Spain, Saarlouis in Germany, Bordeaux in France, Bridgend in Wales and elsewhere began to produce different bits and pieces of Ford cars, and assembly plants all over Europe put them together. After a few years it was impossible to say which country a European Ford car came from. Belatedly GM followed. By the 1980s Vauxhall cars in the UK were simply rebadged Opels, but GM, rather feebly, left its two European brand names in place. So cars led the way, as they so often do in marketing, and since then in many sectors the national walls have slowly been crumbling.

The truck industry is another interesting example of the decline of national flag carriers. Traditionally many European countries, even quite small ones, had their own indigenous heavy vehicle industry. Sisu was Finland's truck company, for instance. Over time in each country one or two dominant players emerged, Leyland in Britain, Berliet in France and Fiat in Italy. Then Fiat, having swallowed Lancia and OM, went on to form a European truck-building business, Iveco. Iveco took over Unic in France, Magirus Deutz in Germany, Seddon Atkinson and Ford Trucks in Britain, all second league national players, and Pegaso in Spain, the national champion. Gradually and with the utmost caution, using the brand name Iveco initially in conjunction with national brand names and then alone, a single brand for trucks emerged. Now the old national brand names have virtually disappeared. Where they exist it's a charade. Volvo Trucks of Sweden owns Renault Trucks. In a field as fraught with national sentiment, prejudice, legal restrictions and traditional dealership patterns as vehicle building, this was quite an achievement.

But nationality never mattered in every single product category. Even in the 1950s and '60s housewives didn't think about where Colgate toothpaste or 'Mild Green Fairy Liquid' dishwashing detergent was made, nor do they very much care where Finish Power Ball toilet disinfectant comes from now. Of course it's true that some domestic habits and practices do vary from country to country. The Danes, Portuguese, British and Poles all wash clothes differently. It's perfectly possible that minor variations in products are required to cope with these differences, but that's a practical rather than an emotional or symbolic differentiation. But women do care a lot about shampoo, conditioner, moisturiser and other very personal products. L'Oréal of France have made rather a corner in this. Their various brands, including Laboratoire Garnier, emphasize a French heritage. How much longer will 'Frenchness', either perceived or real, dominate this sector?

Although it is assumed that computer technology is largely derived from the US, nobody much minds if their PC is made in Ireland, Taiwan or Silicon Valley – as long as it works. One of Apple's largest plants is in Cork, Ireland. Pharmaceutical products come from all over the place and for the most part national origins are ignored. Neutrogena is comparatively unusual in implying that its 'Norwegian Formula' moisturising cream, flourishing a dinky little Norwegian flag on the pack, has national associations and derives from a preparation created for hardy Arctic fishermen. But this kind of fantasy relationship still flourishes in clothing. I have a raincoat branded London Fog. It's made in the Far East and marketed by a North American company. I bought it in London, but the label doesn't fool me, because I happen to be a Londoner and I know that we haven't had fog in London since the 1950s. I presume the idea is that people living in the Mid-West of the US might think it's made for some kind of latter-day Sherlock Holmes striding through a pea-souper, deerstalker in hand and pipe in mouth on his way to solve yet another mystery.

It's all pretty arbitrary. On the one hand Gucci, Armani and Ferrari seem archetypally Italian. On the other hand Agip, whose six-legged dog petrol brand is a ubiquitous sight on Italian roads, has no particular national connotations. Nor does BP tug at British heart strings. The Repsol petrol brand, however, is seen by most Spaniards as a flagship for their nation, although they only have to think about it for a few moments to realize that it can't be very Spanish because the raw material is all imported. Many Finns of my acquaintance choose to believe that around the globe people associate Nokia with Finland and that Finland is therefore regarded as a technological and entrepreneurial paradise. I doubt it. In my experience most non-Finnish people assume Nokia is Japanese and have no views of any kind about Finns and Finland except that it's probably cold up there. In other words, attitudes towards the nation and the brands which derive from it are unpredictable, emotional, variable and spring largely from legend, myth, rumour and anecdote.

This doesn't mean, though, that the connection between the nation and the brand isn't important. On the contrary, country of origin or perceived country of origin still seems to be very significant in purchase decisions. During the 1990s the branding consultancy Wolff Olins joined with the *Financial Times* to carry out a series of studies on what 'Made in…' means. Three separate studies of three different countries were carried out: Britain, Italy and Germany. Over one thousand senior executives from countries around the world were contacted and the results were quite fascinating. Although executives claimed that national origins of products were very important in making purchase decisions, they displayed almost grotesque ignorance about the countries from which they said they bought products. In their answers to questions all their ill-informed and anecdotal prejudices were displayed in full force.

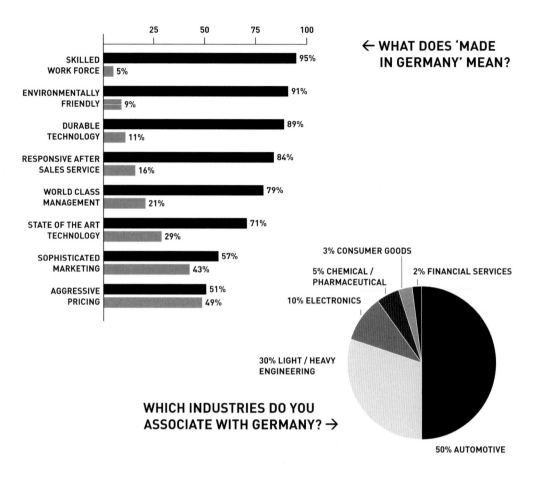

← WHAT DOES 'MADE IN GERMANY' MEAN?

SKILLED WORK FORCE	95% / 5%
ENVIRONMENTALLY FRIENDLY	91% / 9%
DURABLE TECHNOLOGY	89% / 11%
RESPONSIVE AFTER SALES SERVICE	84% / 16%
WORLD CLASS MANAGEMENT	79% / 21%
STATE OF THE ART TECHNOLOGY	71% / 29%
SOPHISTICATED MARKETING	57% / 43%
AGGRESSIVE PRICING	51% / 49%

3% CONSUMER GOODS
5% CHEMICAL / PHARMACEUTICAL
2% FINANCIAL SERVICES
10% ELECTRONICS
30% LIGHT / HEAVY ENGINEERING
50% AUTOMOTIVE

WHICH INDUSTRIES DO YOU ASSOCIATE WITH GERMANY? →

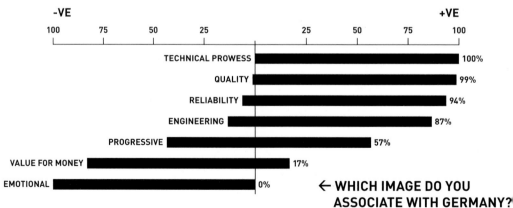

-VE   +VE

TECHNICAL PROWESS	100%
QUALITY	99%
RELIABILITY	94%
ENGINEERING	87%
PROGRESSIVE	57%
VALUE FOR MONEY	17%
EMOTIONAL	0%

← WHICH IMAGE DO YOU ASSOCIATE WITH GERMANY?

For example, Germany was perceived primarily as a country that produces excellent cars, and by extension other engineering products, at high prices. Mercedes Benz, Audi and BMW overwhelm everything else. German marketing skills were regarded as negligible and the emotional characteristics of its products not even worth mentioning. German products were seen to possess an attractive but narrow range of virtues. German achievements in banking, pharmaceuticals, electronics and other areas were largely ignored or unknown. So the picture that emerged was a simplistic caricature of the reality of German industry. The marketing expertise of companies like BMW was ignored. The hi-tech triumphs of SAP were unknown. Major chemical companies like BASF and Bayer were not acknowledged. Deutsche Bank and other German financial institutions might just as well not have existed. German products with a high emotional or style content, such as Nivea, Jil Sander, Hugo Boss, Wella or for that matter Porsche, didn't come into the picture. Because of traditional prejudices created over decades, huge chunks of German industry and commerce appear to derive absolutely no advantage from being perceived as German. Does it matter? Probably. But nothing like as much as it once did. What can be done about it? Well, you can either try to change the way the nation is perceived in the world (see the next chapter) or companies and their products and services that are German and do not fall into the German fantasy picture should perhaps ignore their German origins.

So the picture is much more confused than it seems to be at first sight. Why? First, because it's only some products and services for which national origins are seen to be truly important. Second, because these products and services vary from one country of origin to another. They are mostly but not always personal products – food, drink, clothes, cars and so on – but there are a multiplicity of exceptions. Third, prejudices and ignorance are so great that a self-fulfilling prophecy is almost bound to develop. Potential customers are for the most part increasingly unaware of what is produced where and by whom. So they perpetuate traditional stereotypes: German engineering, Italian fashion and so on.

All this is further confused because as traditional manufacturers move production into countries where costs are lower and more countries move into manufacturing for the first time, established prejudices become more naïve, simplistic and erroneous. All this is happening very quickly and is, for the most part, very little publicized.

For example, the British Royal Air Force has used a primary trainer called the Tucano for some years. The Tucano is marketed by Shorts, historically a great name in British aircraft construction. Shorts built the old Imperial Airways flying boats of the 1930s and the Sunderlands of the Second World War period. Shorts seems like a UK company through and through. So far, so good. But Shorts is owned by Bombardier, a French Canadian defence, aerospace and transport equipment company, and the Tucano primary trainer is built under licence by Shorts in Belfast from Embraer, the Brazilian aircraft design and construction company. Pilots of the British Royal Air Force are learning to fly in Brazilian-designed equipment. Nothing wrong with that. It's fine. Just a bit of a surprise, that's all. But most British people would be amazed to learn that British pilots are trained on equipment of Brazilian origin. Isn't Brazil the land of samba, coffee, carnival and face lifts? What do Brazilians know about aircraft manufacture? As it happens they know a lot. Embraer is one of the world's most successful manufacturers of medium-sized passenger jets. This is an unusual example, but you can find this kind of thing all over the place: Israeli- or Indian-designed software packages, Malaysian-built cars, Turkish washing machines. What does it all mean? How can you make sense of it? The traditional prejudices that even many of the most highly placed executives treasure about which country produces what are much worse than ignorant and anachronistic; they are positively misleading.

It seems to me to be clear that apart from a few sectors – products associated with particular and traditional skills, or products made unique by the nature of the soil (Scotch whisky, Cuban cigars, Burgundy wines and similar idiosyncratic and luxury goods), or anything to do with the arts (film, painting, performing arts and so on) – apart from these sectors, and they are of course influential way beyond their actual size, the real national brand is in terminal decline, while the fantasy national brand Neutrogena (Norwegian), London Fog (British), Baileys (Irish), Häagen-Dazs (Scandi-wegian) is flourishing.

The reality is that traditional national brands are crumbling wherever you look. National airlines are going and national steel companies have gone. Neither the airline easyJet nor the steel company Ispat, the two fastest growing companies in their sector, have any national connotations or associations; in many businesses nationality is a kind of sentimental hangover of no practical value.

So what can companies like Siemens or Sony, whose image is based largely around national character, do? They have to move the emphasis, from 'Siemens – Made in Germany' or 'Sony – Made in Japan' to 'Made by Siemens' or 'Made by Sony', and this has big implications both for the nation and the brand.

The nation and the brands associated with it are deeply entrenched in the collective psyche. The Swedes still sigh over the loss of Volvo Cars to Ford of the US. They regarded Volvo as a national treasure. And the rest of the world buys Volvo cars at least partially because they are seen to embody Swedish values – tough, safe, unshowy but self-confident. Whether Volvo cars are produced in Brazil, Holland, India or China, you can be sure that Ford will seek to maintain what we customers think of as its Swedish heritage. One may be forgiven for thinking that the new BMW-controlled Rolls-Royce car factory at Goodwood in Sussex is intended to be largely a showroom. Where Rolls-Royce cars are actually made may change; where people think they're made may not.

So with a few exceptions that's the way national branding will move – into fantasy land. As in many other aspects of branding perception will matter more than reality.

BRANDING THE NATION

Within a few years...a successful brand
will be seen as a key national asset.

National 'branding' is one of the most contentious political concepts of our time. From Spain to Australia, Denmark to Singapore, many countries are dabbling in it.

The tacit assumption has been that national branding is a novel concept, a shallow substitute for more substantive political projects, of concern only to middle-aged politicians anxious to look young and cool. But this is not true. In reality it is extremely important for a nation's position in the world. As we saw in the last chapter, most people know very little about nations other than their own. Where they know anything at all, their attitudes are formed from myth, rumour and anecdote. These almost always lean towards grotesque caricature which can be bruising to trade, tourism and inward investment. Occasionally, though, ignorance and distortion can become extremely dangerous. The US is without doubt the world's best known country as well as its most powerful and influential, but as it has found to its amazement it is not the best loved. In some parts of the world the United States is deeply disliked. This is a profoundly shocking and disturbing idea for a nation that thinks its values and way of life are the best in the world, and assumes that the rest of the world agrees. It's particularly damaging and distressing for a nation that wants and expects to be admired and liked.

But although the US has massive promotional power and influence, it has never, so far as I am aware, attempted to project a clear co-ordinated idea of itself either domestically or externally. So the outside world's idea of what America is like, what it stands for, what its values are, derives inevitably from the confused, contradictory and extraordinary jumble of ideas that the country exports about itself. America is the cradle of marketing, branding and advertising. It has the world's most powerful media industry – CNN, Hollywood, MTV and the rest of it – so it should be in a strong position to influence its target audiences favourably. But except in times of war or similar external emergency it either doesn't bother, or it isn't able to, because unlike more single-minded states it lacks the means and perhaps the will.

US foreign policy, which is, some might think, at least from time to time, dismissive, arrogant and arbitrary (although I happen to believe that this is a simplistic view), can be a cause of great offence. But another very important factor is the absence of any serious, long-term, consistent attempt on the part of the US to explain, to 'win friends and influence people'.

In this situation three broad strands of thinking have emerged about the US, together with a whole bunch of subsidiary ideas, each of which compete in the minds of non-Americans around the world. They are first, democracy. Land of the Brave, Home of the Free. The Golden Land of Liberty where each individual has an opportunity to achieve wealth and glory. Symbol? The Statue of Liberty. Second, technology. Silicon Valley, Microsoft, Nasa, smart bombs. The nation that leads the world in developing and utilizing technology. Symbol? The PC. Third, seductive junk which undermines and destroys everyone else's national culture. Junk food, McDonald's. Junk drink, Coke. Junk clothes, Nike. Junk entertainment, most of Hollywood. Symbol? All of them.

Each of these concepts jostles about in the minds of the peoples of the world to such an extent that an individual is capable of expressing admiration, love, envy and loathing of the US even in the course of a single sentence. Of course the nature of American society is such that competing, conflicting and complementary currents of opinion and attitude are part of its own reality. So to a certain extent it's not unreasonable to think that the confusion that America projects is a direct reflection of what America is. Nevertheless every American recognizes that he or she is an American, and every non-American recognizes America. By this gauge, if no other, America is a brand.

Two reactions after 9/11.
Above: in the US.
Below: in Pakistan.

It's also undoubtedly the case that all great powers throughout history have provoked envy and jealousy as well as admiration. Britain was not much loved at the time of its imperial zenith in the nineteenth century. Nevertheless the hatred manifested towards the US in the first few years of the twenty-first century inevitably emphasizes the significance of national branding as an important issue. If the US had tried harder, earlier and for longer, to explain itself, would it have been so maligned and attacked?

Interestingly there is nothing particularly novel about the concept of branding the nation. Only the word 'brand' is new. National image, national identity, national reputation are all words traditionally used in this arena and they don't seem to provoke the same visceral hostility as the word 'brand'. Although the technologies are new and infinitely more powerful and pervasive than ever before, and the word 'brand' is also new, the concepts which it encompasses are as old as the nation itself. The Founding Fathers never much cared to influence the rest of the world, nor were they in the early years of the American Republic especially bothered about what other nations thought of them. In this respect, as in many others, the US is atypical. Most nations, however, have devoted obsessive attention, energy and money to building prestige and influence both domestically and externally, and the conscious and deliberate attempt to project a clear, consistent, ideologically dominated national identity has always been central to this activity, so in this sense the US neglect of the external world, an interesting reflection of an isolationist strand in American attitudes, is unusual.

It was the French who really started national branding in a big way. France's five republics, two empires and about four kingdoms (depending on how you count them) offer a fascinating case-study of how creating and establishing identities has been highly influential in establishing their internal legitimacy, their hold on power and their influence on their neighbours.

In the kingdom of the Bourbons nobody was more glorious an autocrat than le Roi Soleil – Louis XIV. Versailles was erected as the physical embodiment of absolute power. Then in 1789 came the first and most significant revolution. Not only was the traditional nobility exiled and dispersed, the royal family executed, a republic proclaimed, religion excoriated, and an entire social and cultural system turned on its head, but every little detail changed too. The Tricolour replaced the Fleur de Lys, the Marseillaise became the new anthem, the traditional weights and measures were replaced by the metric system, a new calendar was introduced, God was replaced by the Supreme Being and the whole lot was exported through military triumphs all over Europe. France was quite consciously and overtly rebranded, the first nation to enter on so self-aware a course. And the whole of Europe was profoundly influenced by it.

Dominic Lieven puts it superbly[1]. 'The revolutionary nationalist doctrine of 1789 was both absolute and abstract. It demanded a far higher level of commitment to the state than was the case in a traditional monarchy…' In other words, the new French republic was much more self-consciously a nation, more aggressive and more determined to create homogeneity – consistency and coherence – than any nation before. And as all of us in the business know, consistency and coherence are what branding is largely about.

Only a very few years later another rebranding operation took place. General Napoleon Bonaparte made himself First Consul, then Emperor. Empire was a concept entirely new and hitherto completely alien to France. Napoleon crowned himself Emperor at his own coronation just like Charlemagne. He introduced new titles, rituals, uniforms, honours and decorations, not to speak of a new legal and educational system which was exported to all his dominions and which has had pretty remarkable staying power. The Napoleonic legal code remains the legal structure in much of Europe today. All this was commemorated and memorialized by a number of artists and writers, of whom Jacques-Louis David was perhaps the most gifted. Under Napoleon, France wasn't big enough; the whole of Europe was rebranded. The accepted view amongst most historians is that this was Napoleon's idea. He may not have been concerned with all the detail, but his was the master plan.

And the rebranding of France has proceeded sporadically and often violently ever since. Napoleon's empire gave way to the restored

Bourbons, who were overthrown and replaced by a bourgeois monarchy, which was followed by a Second Republic, which turned itself into a Second Napoleonic Empire. By the time the Third Republic emerged from the ashes of Napoleon III's defeat at the hands of Prussia, French politicians had become the world's specialists at branding and rebranding the nation.

The Third Republic collapsed in the defeat of 1940 and was replaced by Petain's Vichy. Under Vichy, France was rebranded yet again: the Republican slogan, or as branding experts would put it strapline, 'liberté, egalité, fraternité', was replaced with 'travail, famille, patrie'. Although the Vichy regime is now regarded as a humiliating and shameful period in French history, there is no doubt that it was yet another national brand with, for a short time, a powerful and popular political, cultural and social ideology.

After Vichy came the Fourth Republic and then the Fifth, which is France's current political and cultural incarnation. Of course it's true that there is continuity underneath the change. The French people and France itself continue to demonstrate many traditional characteristics. Nevertheless the brand changes are not superficial, cosmetic or meaningless, they are real and profound. The reason why nations continue both explicitly and sometimes implicitly to shape and reshape their identities, or if you prefer explicitly and implicitly to rebrand themselves, is because their reality changes and they need to project this real change symbolically to all the audiences with whom they relate. They want, so far as they can, to align perception with reality.

I cite the example of France because of all the countries in the world, France is probably the one that has been most influential in the branding and rebranding of other nations. But you can make similar observations about almost but not quite every country.

There was, however, another major influence on nationalism – Germany. Dominic Lieven goes on to talk about nascent German nationalism, '[which] put a heavy stress on ethnicity, and above all language, as the essential defining elements in community identity

… a peasantry that had retained its customs, folk music and languages'[2].

The combination of French revolutionary nationalism and folksy German romanticism – Jacques-Louis David meets Caspar David Friedrich, so to speak – was the starting point for the self-conscious, self-aware nation which emerged throughout the nineteenth and twentieth centuries. National leaders used universal male military service and primary education to create a feeling for national identity that could be shared by all those living inside the nation and respected, admired, feared or at the very least acknowledged by its neighbours.

Bismarck's newly unified Germany, created out of the French collapse of 1870, had an Emperor, a Kaiser. William I, the old, proud Hohenzollern King of Prussia who became under Bismarck's pressure the first Kaiser of the Second Reich, hated the title. He thought it pretentious, bombastic and bogus, unlike his grandson William II, the one who went to war in 1914, who loved being a Kaiser. The newly rebranded Germany, the Second Reich, wallowed in a range of newly reinvented myths, folklore and traditions. Wagner's operatic celebration of Teutonic legends, supported by a panoply of other artists and writers and propagandist historians like Treitschke, reinforced Germany's industrial, economic and military power with a massive cultural presence. Germany was emulated by Italy and eventually by all the new nations in Central and Eastern Europe that emerged from the ashes of the multi-national, multi-lingual Habsburg and Ottoman empires.

Early twentieth-century examples of Nazism in Germany, Fascism in Italy and Communism in Russia (renamed the Soviet Union) are so familiar as hardly to warrant comment – but they were not alone. On the contrary the fashion for national rebranding was widespread.

Atatürk's branding operations in the defeated Ottoman Empire after the First World War rivalled those of the first French

Revolution in scope and scale. They involved a new alphabet, new clothing (all men had to wear smart Western headgear or at least a Turkish version of it), a new name for the nation and all its inhabitants, and perhaps most importantly, in view of recent developments, ethnic cleansing, and a secular rather than a religious state.

Even the British royal family has found it expedient to do a bit of brand building. In 1917, as my colleague Jesus Encinar has pointed out, King George V in the middle of the war with Germany changed the family name from the excessively Teutonic Saxe-Coburg-Gotha to the blandly English Windsor.

'Royal House of Windsor. All German titles dropped.' *Times* headline, July 1917.

After 1945 the collapse of the great European colonial empires created a new wave of nations. Many of those gave themselves new names: Ceylon became Sri Lanka, Gold Coast became Ghana, Southern Rhodesia became Zimbabwe and its capital Salisbury, Harare. The Dutch East Indies became Indonesia. Its capital Batavia was renamed Jakarta and its multiplicity of languages was replaced by the newly coined Bahasa Indonesian. The former Belgian Congo became plain Congo, then Zaire, then Congo again. Entirely new countries like Pakistan and Bangladesh emerged from what had been the British Indian Empire. Bangladesh has had three names in just over half a century; first it was part of India as East Bengal, then it became East Pakistan and then Bangladesh. Each of these new names was a symbol of profound political, economic, cultural and commercial change. Colonial status was swapped for independence. Rebranding the nation was mandatory.

All of these new countries wanted to draw a line and start again. In doing this many of them, like their predecessors in nineteenth-century Europe, uncovered, discovered or invented a pre-colonial heritage; Zimbabwe was a semi-mythical African empire located more or less where present-day Zimbabwe lies. The historical relationship between ancient Zimbabwe and contemporary Zimbabwe is negligible, but the emotional relationship is close.

After 1991, the fall of the Berlin Wall and the collapse of the
Soviet Empire the process began all over again. There were several
new nations carved out of the old Soviet Union itself. Some of
these, like Georgia, had a powerful sense of self and tradition.
Others like Belarus and the five central Asian 'stans' have never
historically existed as independent countries, at least in any kind
of modern sense. They were in effect new nations. Then there
were the three tiny Baltic states of Lithuania, Latvia and Estonia,
always grouped together because they were small contiguous
units with similar recent histories, but of course they saw
themselves as very different from each other; different languages,
religions, ethnicities and cultures. Next were the one-time
independent Central and Eastern European nations:
Czechoslovakia, Hungary, Poland, Romania and Bulgaria. During
this turbulent period Poland created and launched a brand whose
influence still resonates globally although it is now dead within the
country of its birth – a political brand, Solidarnosc (Solidarity),
which emerged fully equipped with all the appropriate
paraphernalia including colours and logo. Yugoslavia was a bit
different; it was Communist but had not recently been Russian-
influenced. Albania was even more peculiar, an isolated, autarkic,
primitive monstrosity. Two of these nations, Czechoslovakia and
Yugoslavia, more or less immediately fell to bits, spawning new,
confused and confusing statelets, while the others in various stages
of disarray tried to shake themselves into life, inventing and
reinventing national myths, legends and history.

The tragic paradox of all this is that while each of these brand new
or newly reinvented nations feels its own nationhood, personality,
strengths, weaknesses and cultural, linguistic, ethnic, religious
and commercial heritage very keenly, for the rest of the world,
especially for the rest of Europe, they are simply, for the most part
at any rate, an undifferentiated, alien, grey porridge. They are new
or newly rebranded nation states which the rest of the world
neither listens to nor cares about, except on occasions when they
momentarily become trouble spots. Then they blink for a moment
in blindingly intense light, which soon disappears, leaving them
languishing again in the dark. The memory of how they impinged

themselves on the public consciousness remains, however. Bosnia, Serbia, Croatia are all remembered in connection with war, savagery and mutual destruction.

It's clear that the urge to create nations remains very strong. Despite the power of corporations and the new regional entities that are emerging, nations remain the defining political unit of our age. There are now more nations in the world than ever before: the UN had 189 members in 2002 compared to 51 in 1945.

Paradoxically, though, the primacy of the nation-state is being questioned, from above by regional integration, from Mercosur in Latin America to NAFTA in North America and above all the European Union, and from below, as regionalism within Spain, Italy, Belgium, Canada, Britain and elsewhere is now joined by regionalism across nations, like the Danish-Swedish Øresund. In the United States many states are trying to assert themselves both politically and economically. In addition countries everywhere are removing themselves from many of their traditional roles in health, education, even security, and letting companies deliver these services instead, which in a sense further undermines their credibility.

Nevertheless in an increasingly competitive world, where there are far more nations than before and where technology offers remarkable promotion opportunities, nations continue to attempt to project their political power, influence and prestige, largely perhaps for their own self-esteem. Nowadays, however, nations also need to compete on hard, quantifiable issues – inward investment, exports and tourism. And this is new. It has never been a major factor historically because tourism was small, inward investment was confined to a relatively few countries and brand export mainly embraced traditional products going to traditional markets. So globalization has changed the game once again. These are issues where there are winners and losers. The winners get richer and stronger, the losers remain poor and weak. Each nation now seeks to promote its individual personality, culture, history and values, projecting what may be an idealized but immediately recognizable idea of itself for economic and commercial as well as political purposes. These pressures drive nations to adopt the marketing and branding techniques used successfully by so many global companies for such a long time.

Most countries start from just about zero because they have little or no recognition. The problem for Belize, Paraguay, Mongolia, Sri Lanka, Honduras and most of the rest of the world's nations is that, outside a very limited sphere, nobody knows or cares anything about them. At the other end of the spectrum, the United States of America stands alone because its world reputation is ubiquitous and overwhelming. Somewhere in the middle are countries like China, India, Russia, Germany, Italy, Britain and France. Although the world has heard of them, perceptions are dominated, as we have seen, by caricature. Spiritual India, efficient Germany, traditional Britain, passionate Spain and so on; distortions which inhibit clear understanding. In fact, it is these well known but often misunderstood countries which have led the way with national branding projects, even though it is the lesser-known nations who may need this even more.

The intensely competitive commercial environment in which the nation-state operates deserves some close attention. Look at inward investment. An increasingly interdependent global economy means that companies have to look outside their own borders to find cheaper places to get their products built. For example, US investment in Mexico has led to *maquiladoras*, US-financed Mexican factories paying Mexican wages for products which are then shipped a few kilometres back across the US border for sale. These *maquiladoras* sustain a significant proportion of the Mexican economy. Nations or regions less conveniently located than Mexico have to fight each other hard to get this kind of investment. Every nation and every region wants to capture the biggest slice of inward investment, from the biggest companies, for themselves. And this means, for example, that Wales may compete with Hungary and Portugal to get major investment from a company in the Silicon Valley, which may be equally ignorant of, or prejudiced about, each or all of them

(I know a man who works in IT in Silicon Valley who thinks that Wales swim in the sea). So prejudice and ignorance have to be dispelled through advertising, brochures, websites, competitive tenders, beauty parades, presentations and all the other paraphernalia of modern marketing.

Marketing inward investment properly is a serious, expensive and sophisticated business. It's about presenting a nation or a region in a powerful, attractive and differentiating way. The presentational and promotional techniques required for this type of activity are similar to those required for marketing products or services. Almost all of the regions and nations successful in attracting investment run sophisticated promotional programmes, have networks of offices around the world and employ professional marketeers. The rewards are considerable. Wales, one of the most successful regions in the world in winning inward investment, attracted $20 billion over eighteen years.

Second, there's export. Corporate brands and the identities of nations from which they derive have always fed off each other and overlapped. I described all this in some detail in the last chapter. Because nationally based brands tend to reinforce stereotypes, they often have the effect of exaggerating an already distorted picture. And this marginalizes vast swathes of a nation's products and services which don't conform to these increasingly irrelevant stereotypes. In addition there are nations, some quite big and well known, which have no clear brand associations at all, like Canada, Turkey or Brazil, but which may be significant manufacturers and exporters of products and services. So if a nation wants to cut through distorting and damaging stereotyping, or wants to be seen to be a force in a field in which it is traditionally little known, it has to use all the techniques of promotion – advertising, exhibitions, trade fairs, national weeks and so on – and rebrand itself.

Finally there's tourism, the world's fourth largest industry, growing at about 9% per year. Some countries depend largely on tourism for their earnings and have developed a sophisticated tourist infrastructure. Many of the most unlikely countries are highly reliant on it. For instance, New Zealand's largest foreign exchange earner is tourism. The danger for countries which rely heavily on traditional tourism is that sun, sea and sand are in danger of becoming a commodity, driven by fierce competition on price into attracting more and more people who often spend less and less money individually. So a country can end up getting large numbers of tourists that it can't effectively cope with, spending very little money per head. The alternative is for countries to trade up, differentiating themselves like consumer brands, emphasizing their art, culture, history, food, architecture, landscape and other unique characteristics through sophisticated imagery. That way the nation will aim to get fewer tourists, each of whom will individually spend more money. There's another emerging problem here, though. Tourists may like a little exoticism but not too many like danger. Egypt, a potentially ideal market for tourists, with a good infrastructure, remarkable historical sites, good swimming and diving, fascinating towns and a strong exotic flavour, is likely to continue to have a tough time while it is associated, whether fairly or otherwise, with terrorism and fundamentalism.

There are a few countries which, through a combination of dramatic political change and the imperative to develop economically, have demonstrated the massive impact that rebranding can achieve.

Advertising campaign from Singapore, 2003, to make the nation look interesting and influential – part of the Singapore branding programme.

The Campo Volantin footbridge in Bilbao, Spain, by Santiago Calatrava.

Spain, once a world power of the first rank, went into a long, self-destructive decline culminating in the hideous Civil War of the 1930s. It degenerated into an isolated, autarkic, poverty-stricken, authoritarian anachronism, hardly part of modern Europe at all. Since Franco's death in 1975, it has transformed itself into a modern, well-off, European democracy. The reality has changed but so have perceptions. Spain appears to have carefully orchestrated and promoted its re-entry into the European family. The extent to which this has been explicitly managed is difficult to determine. Success always makes it easy to post-rationalize and rewrite history, but it certainly didn't happen only through serendipity.

The Joan Miró sun symbol was an identifier for a massive promotional programme closely linked to national change and modernization. Institutional and tourist advertising on a national and regional level, the creation of successful international business schools, the growth, privatization and globalization of Spanish companies like Repsol, Telefónica and Union Fenosa, the rebuilding and beautifying of major cities like Barcelona and Bilbao, the self-mocking, sexually explicit, tragicomic films of Almodovar and his contemporaries, political devolution, the Barcelona Olympics and the Seville International Exhibition of 1992 all underlined and exemplified the change and helped to change perceptions.

Poster for an Almodovar film.

This programme of activities, much based around individual initiatives, has rehabilitated and revitalized Spain both in its own eyes and in the eyes of the world. Spain is among the best examples of modern, successful national branding because it keeps on building on what truly exists; it incorporates, absorbs and embraces a wide variety of activities to form and project a loose and multifaceted yet coherent, interlocking, mutually supportive whole.

Spain is not alone. There are other examples, too: Australia and Singapore, and to a lesser extent Hong Kong and Portugal. Many other national branding programmes are being planned and discussed, although national governments are understandably

Joan Miró's symbol
for Spain.

Josep Maria Trias's
symbol for the 1992
Barcelona Olympic
Games.

reluctant to conduct open discussions on a topic that is complex to explain, wins no votes and can readily invite ridicule.

But, paradoxically, it is those countries which have yet to start that need branding most. The most urgent problems are faced by those nations formerly dominated by the old Soviet Union, like Poland, Hungary, the Czech Republic, the Baltic Republics, Romania and Bulgaria and others that even Western Europeans have difficulty in telling apart. Slovakia and Slovenia are both Slav, small and mountainous, but quite different from each other. Who knows in what ways? It is deeply humiliating for them to be perceived as a single, undifferentiated, anonymous, dreary mass, when in reality they have widely differing languages, ethnic origins, religious affiliations and levels of commercial and industrial development.

Each of these nations of central Europe has an individual history and culture and each of them has a particular personality. Some are quite large (Poland has 40 million people), some are very small (Estonia has 1.5 million, of whom a high proportion are ethnic Russians), but all have changed vastly since they gained the right to choose their own political direction in the early 1990s. These are effectively nations that are unknown except by their immediate neighbours, and yet they have played an extremely important role historically in the European world.

There are other countries, too, much worse off, whose appalling present is sometimes even worse than their frequently miserable past. Take a country like Ukraine. In principle, it could have quite a lot of advantages. It is vast (it has 50 million people) and is a nuclear power with significant mineral and agricultural resources, and even an attractive coastline. In the nineteenth century, as part of Tsarist Russia, Ukraine was a major exporter of high-quality agricultural products, and its Crimean coast was a popular holiday destination. But today exhortations about investing or holidaying in Ukraine have rather a hollow ring. Of course, this is partly because Ukraine's facilities are not up to an acceptable world standard and it is thought to be institutionally corrupt – but so are a lot of countries with a much more attractive image. But if the

reality is wretched, perceptions are even worse. The only
Ukrainian product anybody can recall today is the nuclear fall-out
from Chernobyl. So while Ukraine could become a country on the
global company's investment horizon, with the resources and the
potential for development, it needs to work out how to fulfil it.
The issue for Ukraine is when the brand-building should begin.
If the appalling perception is an accurate reflection of reality, it
may be advisable not to start now. But if the economy won't
improve unless there's investment, and investment depends at
least partly on self-promotion, it may be necessary to get going
quickly. In that case, the key is not to tell lies and pretend things
are better than they really are.

And how many people – apart from real specialists – can tell
the five former Soviet Central Asian 'stans' apart? In reality,
Uzbekistan, Kyrgyzstan, Turkmenistan, Kazakhstan and Tajikistan
are very different. Some are large, some small; some have
huge resources, others don't; some are old-style Communist
dictatorships, others are evolving in a more or less democratic
direction; and of course they all dislike each other. But they've got
a real problem in establishing who and what they are in a world
increasingly cluttered with 'new' nations. Very few new countries
have established a clear brand, let alone a positive one where they
are known for something apart from conflict.

Such countries must eventually realize that in order to be noticed
in the world at large, and to be assisted in the process of change,
rather than lumped together as a bunch of corrupt, useless, self-
destructive basket-cases, they too will have to take active steps
to create a positive identity. Inevitably for these countries such
identities must be based more around opportunities for the
future than today's reality. In this sort of situation a branding
programme can act as a catalyst for change. If they don't launch
such programmes it will be increasingly difficult to attract
attention. They will remain trapped in a morass.

What these countries are just beginning to realize is that they
can adopt similar branding strategies to those which have been

attempted elsewhere – usually by much better-known and better-off countries. There are of course a lot of potential pitfalls, but the basic techniques and approaches are similar. It is only a matter of time before they and virtually every other nation put brand-building on their agendas.

The process of brand-building has already begun in some developed nations. Once it takes off it will become unstoppable. The issue will be where and how to do it successfully and effectively. Managing a branding programme for a nation in the twenty-first century is going to demand a high level of political, managerial and technical skills. If it is too overt, it will be seen as shrill, authoritarian and therefore unpalatable in a citizens' democracy. If it is too low-key it simply won't be seen or heard at all. If it focuses on perceptions at the expense of reality, it will first attract disdain and then indifference. It cannot be conjured up out of thin air: it must draw from reality but it has to be focused, recognizable, coherent and attractive. The most successful national brands are not simply invented, they are based upon a mood, upon the current reality, which they encapsulate and then promote. In this sense they are organic and self-developing. But they need guidance if they are to realize their potential.

In countries with an authoritarian tradition there will be a tendency to impose solutions from above and to coerce or at least put pressure on non-governmental institutions to follow the agreed policy. This would be counterproductive. Nazi and Communist governments of the twentieth century cornered the market in authoritarian propaganda; some of it, like Leni Riefenstahl's films or Italian Fascist architecture, was superb, but the temptation has to be resisted. We don't want any twenty-first-century Riefenstahls making propaganda films about 'The Triumph of the Will'. The essence of new branding programmes is that they capture the spirit of a time and place, and individuals and organizations sense this and join in voluntarily. Compulsion doesn't work because the identity will emerge through a multiplicity of separate messages with some unifying elements, and not just a few single great events.

While a national branding plan is more complex and involves more co-ordination than a commercial identity programme, the essentials are the same. Both commercial and national brand-building are concerned with the creation of clear, simple, differentiating propositions often built around emotional qualities which can be readily symbolized both verbally and visually. These propositions must be easy to understand and sufficiently flexible to operate in a wide variety of situations with a large number of audiences.

Governments can create the mood and lead and co-ordinate the programme. Coherent efforts within every department – culture, arts, sport, industry, education, transport and environment and, of course, foreign affairs – can stimulate, inspire and steer. There has to be a powerful visual focus, an agreement to make it work and an adequate power base and funding.

There are many pitfalls to avoid. A government planning to launch a branding programme should:

- Set up a working party with representatives of government, industry, the arts, education, sport and the media. The working party should be properly funded with an effective power base. The working party should then appoint consultants to guide the programme.

- The working party or a small steering group of the whole should identify and define critical audiences. Research should be carried out to examine how the nation is perceived both by its own people and by particular target audiences in other nations.

- The working party should develop a process of consultation with opinion-leaders to look at national strengths and weaknesses, compare them with the results of the internal and external research studies, and look at a number of options for core ideas.

- It should then create the core idea on which the national brand will be based and from which the entire programme should be developed. This must be visualized through colours, a symbol, typography. It's at this juncture that a prominent artist should be commissioned to create the national icon. Joan Miró's sun symbol for Spain is perhaps the admired model. It would be desirable to identify a potential major project which could have global significance and which would draw attention to the nation, like the Seville Exhibition or the Barcelona Olympics did for Spain.

• A brand book should be developed, illustrating and demonstrating the national mood, personality and style. This book could be used as a model by different enterprises within the nation which want to project an idea of themselves related to the national imagery.

• Messages required for the very different but complementary sectors, inward investment, export and tourism, should be co-ordinated and modulated so that they are appropriate for each audience and so that they reflect the central idea.

• Over a period everything produced by or representing the nation, from tourism promotions and airlines to products and services, should be co-ordinated so that anything that comes from the nation is readily recognizable.

• The working party should seek to influence the influencers. It should create a liaison system through appropriate organizations in commerce, industry, the arts, media and so on. The programme as a whole will get major coverage from influencing the people who themselves exercise influence and form opinions in their different fields, both at home and abroad.

The project should then be rolled out gradually without making a big song and dance. This means looking at every opportunity. Not just the obvious things like trade fairs, advertising and commercial work in embassies. People are influenced by food, film, art, sport as well as more obvious and direct forms of promotion. That's why film festivals and football matches (especially if the nation wins) are quite as significant as commercial missions.

The key is to get a clear idea, make the programme manifest by visualizing it and implementing it in all those official, unofficial and influential activities where it is possible and credible, and in this way to create or co-ordinate a movement which leading organizations and individuals outside government circles join because it suits them. In Britain, the National Health Service, a great and much loved institution currently at less than its formidable best and a massive employer, could, if it got its act together sufficiently, become highly influential in helping to build a British brand. The example of Spain is significant. The clothes designer Adolfo Dominguez, the film-maker Alejandro Amenabar, and the architect and engineer Santiago Calatrava are not government hacks hired by the hour. They are world-class figures whose work shares the courage and optimism of the new Spain, partly at any rate because over many years the Spanish government in the centre and regional governments have worked hard at creating and projecting a bold and optimistic vision, based on a reality of change, which inspired them and in which they shared.

All countries communicate all the time. They send out millions of messages every day through political action or inaction, through popular culture, through products, services, sport, behaviour, arts and architecture. Collectively, all these millions of messages represent an idea of what the nation as a whole is up to, what it feels, what it wants, what it believes in. It should be the task of government – with a very light touch – to set the tone for these messages, and to lead by example where appropriate so that something credible, coherent and realistic can emerge.

Within a few years, brand management will be seen as a perfectly normal manifestation of what is now called joined-up government. A successful brand will be seen as a key national asset. No country will be able to ignore the way the rest of the world sees it. Politicians everywhere in the world now realize that every nation has an identity: they can either seek to manage it or it will manage them. Let the example of the United States be a clear warning.

HOW TO CREATE AND SUSTAIN A BRAND
SOME GUIDELINES

Overall because branding is about creating and sustaining trust it means delivering on promises. The best and most successful brands are completely coherent. Every aspect of what they do and what they are reinforces everything else.

CHAPTER 9

PREVIOUS PAGES
**Sign in a London street
for a furniture restorer.**

From the outside branding looks simple. It seems to involve the irritatingly frequent, sometimes obsessive repetition of a simple, often extravagant claim expressed through a strapline or slogan, some colours and a distinctive logo, plastered apparently more or less at random on everything in sight. In reality, though, like most things, when you get close up branding isn't quite so simple after all. In fact it's very complex.

There are many different kinds of brands. Fast moving consumer goods like Pepsi and Mars bars still dominate the mindset of most people when they think about brands and these are straightforward products with no service element. But nowadays an increasing number of very popular brands are service-dominated and even some major consumer brands like Burger King or Starbucks have a mixture of product and service elements, which makes them particularly challenging to manage. Then there is the traditional division between business to business and business to consumer brands.

Another category distinguishes between invented and reinvented brands. Invented brands have been newly created like, say, the communications services brand Ono in Spain or the Hutchison 3G video phone, whose brand is simply called 3. Reinvented brands have mutated over long periods of time or been recreated to look new. Two such brands from Spain are Repsol and Telefónica, both of which changed and grew as Spain's economic influence expanded towards the close of the twentieth century, until they became Spanish commercial flagships. Germany's RWE, which is now one of the world's largest utilities involving gas, water and electricity companies in many different countries, has mutated from an old-style traditional electricity utility in Germany's Ruhr.

Then there are corporate brands. This category is becoming increasingly significant as their different audiences – partners, suppliers, investors, shareholders, governments and customers – overlap and intertwine. As people become better educated, more sophisticated and less deferential, they become increasingly interested in the company behind the brand, so corporate brands tend to have high visibility. Those such as Wal-Mart, Nokia or Boeing address every audience of the organization, including the final consumer. Stelios Haji-Ioannou's brand easy, which started with easyJet but now has easyCar, easyValue and easyMoney, represents the new kind of organization which emphasizes how it does things rather than what it does – attitude rather than product.

Brands, as I have pointed out already, have expanded way beyond the business world. There are not-for-profit brands like YMCA, academic brands like Yale, sporting brands like Juventus and arts brands like Britain's Tate. Increasingly there are attempts to brand places. Sophia Antipolis near Cannes is a hi-tech park, almost a region, and has many of the characteristics of a brand. There are city brands, regional brands and even the nation as a brand.

There are brands which express one simple, readily comprehensible message: *Vogue* magazine in its various national manifestations means high fashion. There are other brands, an increasing number in fact, which embody a mix of complex and apparently contradictory ideas, like, say, Oxford University.

With all these divisions and sub-divisions, together with a lot more that I haven't yet attempted to describe, it's not surprising perhaps that classifying brands and branding, when you get close up, is formidably complex.

Building a successful brand is not easy. Many new brands fail. But once a brand has been launched and established it can be maintained almost indefinitely provided that it is properly looked after and husbanded. Even a series of determinedly self-destructive managements have failed to destroy MG Cars, though the great accounting firm Andersen committed suicide by committing the cardinal sin of breaking trust and colluding with its client Enron in fraudulent practice. And creating and sustaining trust is what branding above everything is all about. Unilever is culling its brands. In 2000 it had 1,600 brands worldwide. In 2004 it will have 400. It has killed some brands and sold others to a mix of companies who think they can do better with them.

Many organizations seem to have difficulty in understanding what a brand is and where it begins and ends, let alone trying to work out how to create it, how to position it, how to promote it, how to control it, how to monitor its performance, how to grow it, how to sustain its personality and character and – above all – how to make money out of it. It's tough enough with product brands where a considerable body of knowledge has been built up over more than a century, but with service brands, where corporate experience is far smaller and organizational structures are frequently so ineffective, it's even harder. The reason why so many brands fail is because creating and sustaining a brand demands skill, courage, money, determination, originality, creativity and an infinite capacity to take pains, and that is a rare combination.

Of course there are all kinds of rules and formulae about creating and maintaining brands: if you want to know what they are there are plenty of websites to scan and books to read. The only reliable rule to remember, though, is that no rules are universally applicable. The branding world is full of exceptions – and no formula, however superficially attractive and all-embracing, can do it for you. Branding by numbers, like painting by numbers, only takes you so far.

And what's more, although the principles remain the same, every single branding problem is different. During the 1970s the design and branding consultancy Wolff Olins, of which I was then Chairman, was working both for Renault and Volkswagen. I was deeply involved in both jobs (incidentally it wasn't a conflict of interest – both companies knew we were working for the other) and we advised each company to adopt completely different branding strategies. Why? Because there were an infinity of issues to do with positioning, corporate history, distribution patterns, the market and so on which led us into

recommending diametrically opposite solutions for the two
direct competitors.

Overall, because branding is about creating and sustaining trust,
it means delivering on promises. The best and most successful
brands are completely coherent. Every aspect of what they are
and what they do reinforces everything else. Wherever you touch
a coherent brand, as a customer, a supplier, a shareholder, an
employee, it feels the same. The best brands have a consistency
which is built up and sustained by people inside the organization
who are immersed in what the brand stands for.

In this book I have kept references to Mission, Vision and Value
statements to a minimum, although I am aware that they form the
basis from which most organizations seek to project a clear idea to
their staff and other stakeholders about who they are, what they
stand for, what they are there for and where they are going. I've
read literally hundreds of these and I've also written or helped to
write quite a few and with the best will in the world I can't think
that they are much use. For the most part I find them pious,
predictable, repetitive, interchangeable and ultimately irrelevant.
I once showed the board of a pharma company five mission
statements from their own company and from competitors and
not one single board member could pick out his own company's
mission statement from the rest of the pack.

Not all companies are driven by the high-minded waffle that
their mission statements proclaim. Many are driven by peer
group pressure, envy, ambition and other unlovely but real
human emotions. Just to take one example, what's the real
mission of Komatsu? Simple. Beat Caterpillar. But they don't
feel comfortable putting that in writing.

That's why I much prefer brand books which, when they are well
written and illustrated, convey the style, tone, personality and
idiosyncrasies of an organization by words and pictures and
through analogy, example and nuance. The brand book can
be large or small, mainly words or mainly pictures; it can have

detailed instructions on how to manifest the technical aspects of the identity or it can ignore these, but it must always characterize the organization, so that whoever picks it up and looks at it recognizes that this is what the organization is all about.

And that's why I have focused on coherence, consistency and a powerful emotional idea or attitude, sometimes called a core idea, or a Big Idea, as my basis for brand strength. Brand books, when they are really good and highly individual, can effectively encapsulate the corporate personality, aims and attitudes in an engaging fashion. Above all, people recognize the organization from them.

Although I deeply distrust rules, I find slightly to my surprise that I have worked out some for myself. They are perhaps guidelines rather than instructions. For the rest of the chapter I outline and elaborate on these. They do not purport to explain the entire process of branding from beginning to end, but they suggest a methodology – a way of thinking and working which has at least helped me. Other people have no doubt worked out other systems.

Guideline One – The four vectors

For me the clearest way to start understanding a brand is to look at it through the four vectors by which it manifests itself. These are: product, environment, communication and behaviour. You might say they are the brand's four senses. I have written about this many times before but, because it's the base, the place where I start, I hope it does no harm to repeat it.

The product is what the organization makes or sells. Environment is where it makes or sells it. Communication is how it tells people, every audience, about itself and what it's doing. And behaviour is how it behaves – and that of course means how every single person who works inside the brand comports himself or herself in any interaction of any kind with any other individual or organization. The comparative significance of each of these vectors varies according to the nature of the brand.

Anything that's made is a product-led brand. Toyota, like all car companies, is product-led: it's the product that's at the core of the brand. What the car looks like, feels like to sit in and drive, how much it costs, how much fuel it uses, how the doors sound when you open and shut them, what the neighbours think when it's parked outside the front door and a thousand other things about the product itself affect our purchase decision. In a product-led brand, function, that is how and how well the product works, is of course important but this is supported by other aspects of product design. Ergonomic and aesthetic design allied to function is the key to success. Increasingly, as we saw in Chapter 2, product design is carefully crafted to exploit and manipulate our emotions. But even in product-led brands the other vectors remain important. Communication, environment and behaviour, especially sales and service behaviour, are all key factors in automobile marketing. Companies dominate their dealers' showrooms, manufacturers' brand identities on fascias, signs and interiors making it clear who is boss. Automobile companies are also major advertisers all over the world, so all the vectors of branding are vital. But if the product isn't right you can forget the rest.

Environmental factors in branding are increasingly being called 'brand experiences'. There isn't anything new about this. Environments and the experiences they provide have always been important. It's just that in the first period of branding – up to, say, 1970 – environments didn't really enter the brand developer's mindset. All food markets everywhere are environmentally led. They are fun to walk around. Go to a fish market in a port early in the morning. It's a joyful experience. Exactly the same factors apply in some department stores. They're nice places to be in. You can walk around them, jostle with and stare at other customers, have a coffee or a snack, handle the merchandise and buy if you feel like it. You don't have to rush. That's why so many department stores are environmentally led brands. Supermarkets, despite resistance from their financial people with their focus on sales per square metre, are also moving in this direction. Most hotels are, too. We choose hotels (apart from the price) because of what it feels like to be in them, what facilities they have and where they are

located. All these are environmental factors. Property developers, at least the more imaginative ones, are realizing that developing the property into a brand is going to give it a particular cachet. In Belfast, where the Titanic was built, in fact in the very docks where the ship was constructed, the city's largest property development including 'housing, leisure, heritage and cultural uses' is under way. The area is to be called the Titanic Quarter and the letterhead will carry 'the distinctive four-funnel logo'[1].

Some people unconsciously, or at least subconsciously, choose predictable environments. Most Holiday Inns are pretty much the same, which is why a lot of people choose to stay in them. So if some of us go somewhere strange or new, whether it's Augsburg or Atlanta, we might seek the environmental reassurance that a Holiday Inn can offer. On the other hand, there are many people who look for special and particular environments. All the new, small, minimalist smart hotels designed by the Philippe Starck brigade of designers and featured in 'Hip Hotels' guides are environmentally led.

Above: a stall in the market place in Toulouse, France, full of life and vigour. Below: a supermarket shelf – a bit plasticky.

My favourite hotel, the Ciragan Palace in Istanbul, doesn't have the best food or service of any hotel I know but it does have the most extraordinary site and an overwhelming environment. Well, it should. It was designed as an Ottoman palace and put down on the shores of the Bosphorus on the edge of two continents. In hotels it's the environment that leads the brand. Of course communication, behaviour and product matter. Nobody would go to a hotel twice, however beautifully designed, furnished and located, if the food and service were lousy. But it is the environment that sets the tone.

Fmcgs like Coca-Cola, Kellogg's Corn Flakes and Persil, the products we traditionally associate with the word 'brand' itself, are always communication-driven. Specifically they are advertising-driven. Red Bull, the newish energy drink which stems from the unlikely alliance of Austrian and Thai interests, is a classic fmcg, and like the rest of them is led through communication – packaging, events, display material and so on, although funnily

enough, not a lot of advertising. The name, colours and logo are designed to arouse a particular set of emotions. But it's the emotional stance of the product seen through its communications that's key.

To take a much more extreme example of drinks brands that are communication-led, look at bottled water. Why is bottled water so fashionable? Water is, we are told, very good for us. We should drink lots of it. But why does it have to be imported into, say, Japan from France, Italy or the Highlands of Scotland? Does this kind of water taste so very different from local water out of a tap? Not really. Some people claim they can tell the difference. But after just one gulp? Doubtful. Even if it has bubbles they're often added by machine. But bottled water has emotional connotations of health, purity, activity and fitness which seem to have a special resonance for the Western world. And very many people, including me, are perfectly prepared to pay relatively large sums of money for the emotional satisfaction they derive from drinking it. It's primarily communication that makes Badoit, Perrier and the rest so successful.

When you package it effectively, you can even sell water expensively. Water from Scotland, Italy, France and Wales.

One of the reasons why so many people have a visceral dislike of branding is because they believe, quite correctly, that communication in branding is often manipulative and misleading. What these critics forget is that most people who buy brands are not half-witted and they know that. They also know perfectly well what they are doing. Put in the bottled water context, we buy it because it makes us feel good. In other words, most of us who are persuaded by advertising or other forms of promotion into making a purchase are quite aware at one level or another that the marketing people are attempting to exploit our various insecurities. But we are quite content to go along with them. It's collusive.

In all three of these vectors design is the driving force. You can see the brands, feel them, touch them, clamber all over them, walk around them. That's why so many emerge from a design background. Any product, like an electric shaver or a pair of shoes or a watch, depends on design to make it look and feel different. The same is true of bottled water, where the shape and colour of the bottle are so influential. It's also true of environmentally led brands. Selfridges, the London department store, came back to life after it was totally redesigned. Communication design plays a large role in service brands. Look at the cell phone company Orange. But Orange is, despite expert communication, behaviourally led. Which brings us to the fourth vector. Behaviour comes from a different root. You can't design it. You can't see it or feel it or touch it, although you can sometimes hear it and you can certainly sense it. Most brands nowadays involve behaviour.

Every kind of service that we buy is behaviourally driven or influenced. Supermarkets and other retailers have a large behavioural element, as do airlines and financial services; so do hotels, of course. There's hardly anything that we come into contact with, from health to communication to transport to holidays to business or academic institutions, that doesn't involve a massive behavioural element, usually associated with one or more of the traditional design elements. Hospitals are a very interesting mix. Product clearly matters. We wouldn't want to go to a hospital where the surgeons had a record of disaster. But environment and behaviour are what we deal with as patients – and are what our reactions are largely based on. It's what our ward or room looks like and on how the nurses behave that we tend to make judgments. Airlines are also a classic example of behaviourally led brands. We almost always judge an airline on the basis of the service we received; not how long it took to go from Budapest to Amsterdam but what the experience was like from the moment we arrived at the airport till the time when we picked up our luggage.

Perhaps the most significant behaviourally led brand that most of us come in contact with at one time or another is a police force – or service as they now prefer to be called. The Los Angeles Police Department gained its deeply disagreeable reputation through a series of incidents involving bad behaviour which couldn't be denied because they were videoed. Every police department everywhere in the world is judged almost exclusively on the way it behaves. Unfortunately on this criterion there aren't that many that come up smelling of roses.

But almost all brands are a mix of these four vectors. A police department may be behaviourally dominated, but product matters a lot. Are the police efficient? Do they catch villains? Are crime figures going down?

Disney is perhaps the classic example of a very clever, sophisticated brand that uses all four vectors very powerfully. The Disney organization has been heavily criticized. It overpays its Chief Executive. It is ruthless, even savage to people who get in its way. It is not, as I write, financially all that successful, but it knows how to create and sustain brands. Disney's branding reaches its apotheosis in its theme parks, a complex and carefully modulated mix of product, communication, environment and behaviour. Supermarkets are also an interesting mix of product, environment, communication and behaviour. Look at Wal-Mart. An obsessive focus on choice, consistent quality, knock-down prices and an overwhelmingly cuddly service.

Even unlikely brands are mixing all four vectors. Although not a traditional fmcg brand, Nike has for many years behaved like one; it is of course communication- and product-led. Running shoes are products. They are designed with great care, and every detail of their construction and appearance is carefully monitored. The sophistication of Nike's communications is legendary – in some quarters you might say notorious – but Nike has now built a series of monuments to itself called Niketown. So Nike sportswear is somehow embracing environments too.

As the world in which brands operate becomes more complex, as the media they use become more competitive, brands are going to have to work very hard to look for a place in the consumer's soul. What this means is that over the next few years most brands will use most vectors.

Guideline Two – Brand architecture

When I first wrote about what I called 'brand structure' in the 1970s I described three options.

The first option was corporate (which I called 'monolithic'), where one name and visual idea is used to describe everything the organization does – the corporate brand – like Nokia, Lego and Tesco. Some Japanese and Korean companies have a particular tradition of calling virtually everything they do, quite regardless of what it is, by one name: Yamaha pianos and motorcycles all come from the Yamaha organization. Mitsubishi cars, aircraft, canned food and banks come from a much more loosely knit group of companies with interlocking interests and a related history largely held together by a single name.

The second option was 'endorsed', where an organization has a series of brands, each of which has its own name and identity, but which are also seen as part of a whole like, say, Balliol College or Saïd Business School at Oxford University; or in the industrial world United Technologies with its separate, well known manufacturing and marketing units, Pratt & Whitney, Sikorsky and so on. Or in the hotel and restaurant business there is Accor which now endorses many of its brands with its corporate name, from upmarket Sofitel to not-many-frills Mercure.

The third option I called 'branded'. In the branded structure each unit or brand is projected separately to the consumer and is seen to be completely independent, although the reality of course is that it is owned by an entity which manages, controls, markets, distributes it; an example is Diageo with Guinness, Johnnie Walker, Baileys, Smirnoff, Pimms, Tanqueray and others.

These three options outline the broad principles, but of course in real life there are a multitude of subtle variations on each of these categories, which can be adapted to suit the corporate purpose[2]. In the world of brand architecture most companies, unsurprisingly, follow the orthodoxy of their sector and regard every deviation from it as tantamount to commercial suicide. So Shell, whose identity is based around a corporate structure, would never seriously consider developing stand-alone brands, although from time to time various Shell units toy with the idea. Unilever, on the other hand, would be unlikely to move towards a corporate branding structure because its world outlook, organization and commercial relationships are all based around distinctive and separate brands, and have been for more than a century. Unilever brands are culled from time to time, and the company is considering, like Nestlé, endorsing them with the Unilever name but nothing much has happened as I write in 2003. This attitude of 'what we currently have works best for us' – to put it another way, 'if it ain't broke, don't fix it' – is usually but not invariably sensible.

Some organizations, though, use too many brands and not enough endorsement, and simply waste money. Centrica, the UK services company, is admirable in many ways but it owns a series of brands, including British Gas, the Automobile Association and the credit card Goldfish, each of which is marketed entirely independently of the other. Why? Because the company is dominated by the fmcg model – in my judgment inappropriately for this business. If Centrica adopted an endorsed model there might be useful referred business from one brand to another from the satisfied customer. More importantly, investors, potential recruits and the rest of us would be much less confused.

Electrolux, the Swedish consumer durables company, owns (as I write) a multitude of brands and its main problem, in marketing terms at least, is corporate confusion and inordinate waste. According to the *Economist*, 'As things stand, this plethora of brands is a problem. Electrolux must maintain many complicated manufacturing operations to support them.'[3] Electrolux needs drastically to rationalize its branding and it seems as though it's trying to deal with the problem.

The rule to remember in brand structure is that everything being equal the fewer brands you have the better – because it's simpler and cheaper to use one brand rather than several. Of course in reality things never are equal, so you have to choose the option that works best in a given situation. I talked earlier in this chapter about two different structural models for Renault and VW. Renault use a corporate model, although with a significant investment in and management control of Nissan this is somewhat modulated, while VW use a branded model. Which works better? Nobody knows. You can't do it twice.

In the high-fashion world, Armani, Versace and Chloé have found it appropriate to use the branded structure. We all want to believe that the brands we choose have been specially and exclusively created for us in small workshops lurking down quaint alleyways in old European cities. The idea of course is to persuade us that each of these brands has retained its traditions and integrity, and that it is in touch with its roots.

Deciding whether the brand structure or architecture is corporate, endorsed or branded is just as big a decision as the product/communication/environment/behaviour mix. Of course it's sensible to look at what other companies in the sector do, but in the end each individual decision has to be taken on its particular merits.

Guideline Three – Invented, reinvented and name changes

Is the brand invented or reinvented? That shouldn't be too difficult a problem to resolve, at least in principle. If it's there already, if it exists, if people work for it, if it has recognition and for one reason or another it has to be changed, then it's a reinvented brand. If it's new, it's just an idea in somebody's head, it has no reality, then it has to be created and it's an invented brand. There's a very big difference between these two. When you invent a brand there is no business, nobody works for it, there isn't an office, you start literally with a blank sheet of paper. But when you reinvent a brand it's quite different; there already exists a culture, a tradition, an attitude and a reputation, often a very longstanding one. And there's also a name. There are employees, customers, shareholders, suppliers. How much can you or should you change? If the entire organization is moving in a new direction – merging, acquiring, divesting, being privatized, going through massive technological and cultural change or something similar – the probability is that the whole organization will need to shift and be seen to shift. It will need to be reinvented. Sometimes names have to be changed.

That's what happened with the merger between the two utilities giants Viag and Veba in Germany. They merged and, although they stayed in the same business more or less, everything else changed. E.on was intended to be more than a new name for two old rivals that had merged. The new brand encapsulated a reinvented organization with new loyalties and a new culture. That's very often why name changes, so frequently vilified in the media, take place. Two old rivals merge and a new entity must be created.

Name changes are perhaps the most sensitive and certainly the most contentious of all branding issues, at least in the minds of the media and the public. Most companies will go to very great lengths to avoid changing names. Name changes are expensive and complex and they are almost always publicly ridiculed when they are first announced. But sometimes it just can't be helped. And anyway after the first few weeks of irritation, it all goes away, everyone gets used to the new name and that's the end of it.

Viag plus Veba equals e.on: a massive German brand.

When Andersen Consulting finally broke with its auditing parent, then called Arthur Andersen, and both organizations went their separate ways, the agreement was that Andersen Consulting would have a new and different name, hence Accenture launched in January 2001, which was of course subjected to a brief but lively campaign of mud slinging. In retrospect it's clear that this was probably the best decision Andersen Consulting ever made. The new brand probably saved them from extinction. Accenture has not been tarnished in any way by the collapse, humiliation and disgrace of its former stablemate. But imagine the impact if it had still been called Andersen Consulting. So changing names isn't always so silly after all. In fact sometimes it's very sensible.

Most venerable brands are of course adapted or reinvented from time to time, sometimes on a regular basis. Some time-honoured brands, like Lufthansa or Marmite or Mastercard, are continually being modulated or revised or adapted to cope with new or changing circumstances, new products or services, or to anticipate new requirements or demands from the market place. If the people running the organization are smart enough and sensitive enough, many of the modulations in branding won't need to be overt, they'll just keep on happening and be absorbed into the bloodstream of the business. Over decades Michelin, Nestlé, Deutsche Bank, Pfizer and others have subtly modified their identities to keep themselves in the same place.

Invented brands are different. They start from scratch. When Daimler Benz teamed up with Swatch, the people who changed the Swiss watch industry, to create a new small town car that could go and park anywhere, there was a real new branding issue. The car could of course have been called Mercedes or Swatch, but the product was quite unlike any other. It was produced in purpose-built factories, it had its own staff with their own unique culture, it had its own distribution system. And above all it had nothing to do with traditional car values. It looked different, its pricing was different, its market was different, so it became a new brand – Smart.

It's only when something major happens, like the new Smart car, or a new kind of distribution system in financial services, like First Direct or Egg, that the issue of a new or reinvented brand comes up. First the big and basic decisions are made, and then whether you invent or reinvent are matters of judgment.

Guideline Four – Product quality

When you launch or relaunch a brand, you have to be clear about product quality. If your product is as good as the best there is in terms of price, quality and service, that gives you a licence to take part in the race. If your product is better than anything else around, don't get too relaxed because you can be sure that your competitors will catch up – usually very quickly. If your product is not as good as the best you will certainly fail.

In the cell phone market Nokia is winning because for a long time its phones have been easier to use and better looking than its competitors, especially Motorola and Ericsson. These two companies have lost massively in market share because their products haven't been as good as the best. Now Motorola and Sony Ericsson make very competitive products and they are trying to catch up. But it may be too late.

Guideline Five – The inside and the outside

The basic rule of marketing is that the final customer comes first. Unless you understand and woo your final customer you're dead. Ever since marketing first swept across the North Atlantic from the US to Europe on a tidal wave of detergents, breakfast food and fizzy drinks this has been the unchallenged rule.

But now that service branding is becoming so important, things have changed. Although it remains true that brands will die without customers, it's also true that lousy service brands will kill themselves, because their staff will undermine and destroy the customer base. In a service brand the most important audience for the organization is its own people. Your staff must truly understand the brand, believe in it and live it; if they don't they will have no chance of persuading the final customer to buy it.

I always remember the tale of a friend who wanted a Mercedes. He went to a Mercedes dealership metaphorically clinking the cash in his pocket. But the salesman who tried to sell him a car smelled of drink. My friend found him obnoxious – pressing and unpleasant. He disliked the experience so much that he invented reasons to buy another make of car. He asked people in his neighbourhood what they thought of the dealer's service. He heard bad stories. He still thought Mercedes were fine, but he persuaded himself that Audi was a better product. He bought an Audi instead.

What's the moral of the little tale? Brands have two roles – persuading outsiders to buy and persuading insiders to believe. The Mercedes dealer visited by my friend didn't manage its people properly. The dealer didn't realize that brands are about both the inside and the outside. One of the many messages in this book is that in service brands the people who work for the brand have to live and breathe it. Because for the customer they are the brand.

Guideline 6 – Differentiators or core ideas

Your product or service needs to be differentiated. There must be something about it that is unusual, even unique. Sometimes it's a Big Idea perceived through design which creates difference. A product is designed to be prettier, lighter, or smaller, or easier to use, or to appeal to a specific market. Toys are a classic example of differentiation through design. Lego uses product design to establish aesthetic differentiation and brand personality. So does Playmobil.

Most successful brands have a clear and simple idea which sets them apart. Ryanair, for example, represents cheap in the fullest possible meaning of the word. Differentiation can sometimes emerge through creativity in communication. Absolut Vodka is absolutely obsessive, but it's absolutely witty too. The best differentiating ideas are immediately recognizable.

But differentiation can be strangely elusive to discover. Some years ago I was working on a Wolff Olins project with the Portuguese Tourist Board to market Portugal as a tourist destination. Most tourists from Northern Europe went on package holidays to the Algarve, the southern coast of Portugal, for sun, sea and sand. But sun, sea and sand have become commodities. In order to differentiate Portugal as a tourist destination we had to find a core idea that was real, recognizable and marketable, and that set Portugal apart. At one level of course Portugal was just another Latin European holiday destination, superficially perhaps not so very different from France, Italy or Spain. So what did differentiate Portugal? The answer was so simple and so obvious, so important and so real, that once we had seen it, we didn't see how we could ever have missed it. Portugal, unlike the rest of Latin Europe, is not a Mediterranean country; its coastline is Atlantic. The sea is cold.

It has waves; big ones. Traditionally Portugal doesn't look at Europe. It looks outward across oceans. You can see that in its geography and history. The differentiating idea for Portugal is that it is a Southern European country on the Atlantic. Everything followed from that.

When you've got the core idea you have to give it creative life. It always needs to be designed, given names, colours, typefaces, a powerful visual style, sometimes music or even smells, from which it derives emotional power. There has been so much written about design, some of it by me, that I am disinclined to add much more. Just this, though: in a visually sophisticated age, with competition increasing exponentially and products/ services becoming increasingly similar, design remains the great differentiator. Design always has been an immensely influential power in creating differentiation and it always will be.

Guideline Seven – Breaking the mould

Occasionally, when the brief calls for an entirely new product or service, it may be an opportunity to reject the existing conventions that surround a business and go for something entirely new.

When Apple came into the computer business in 1976 it broke the mould. The computer conventions had been set by IBM – name, colours, shapes, the ponderous, conservative marketing machine. The whole style of IBM in the 1970s was encapsulated in the nickname Big Blue. The entire industry tried to be IBM. For a time Honeywell called itself 'the other computer company'. The UK company ICL even tried to sound like IBM. Then Apple came into the market with a new product, a new name and visual style, a much more joyful, intriguing and friendly new product and set of rules, and it broke the mould. Computing was never the same again. For a time the computer world became an orchard: there was Apricot, Peachtree and whole rows of others. But they didn't last. It was Apple that had done it.

Breaking the mould usually, but not always, happens through design. But sometimes the business model is different. In home furnishings retailing IKEA broke the mould with a very simple idea[4]. If you make the customer do most of the work and are quite upfront about offering a lower level of service, you can sell the product for less – an innovative idea, creatively marketed.

Guideline Eight – Reducing risk - research

Executives spend much of their time trying to reduce risk. But all branding is about risk. So how can you reduce risk in branding? What about research? How useful is it? What does it tell you? Research is extremely useful if you want to know how big the market is, what people currently think and feel about the products in it and so on. Good research, and there is now a lot of good research around, can tell you a lot about consumer trends, what consumers feel about the products and services they buy, and what they feel about the world around them. In other words research will tell you a lot about the past and current situation. It can give you a fair indication of what people are moving towards emotionally. Once you've launched a product or service, it will tell you what went wrong and what went right. It will tell you whether the product was properly priced, whether it was available generally, what people felt about the advertising, what people felt about how the product works – everything.

The only thing that research, at least in my experience, can't help you with is the bit in the middle. Will your product work in the market place? Will it sell? Will people like it? If research could help to get that part right, there would be no failures. But that's just where research can't help. I have been associated in my lifetime with quite a few successes and also some pretty big failures. We always found it quite easy to find out what had gone wrong afterwards. Research told us a lot about what we should have done, about how if we had modified the formula, or achieved wider distribution, or slightly reduced the price, things would have been different. But research was never able to help us with these issues before we launched.

Much research is extremely useful, especially on a macro level. But don't rely on it too much for your micro activities. Research is not a crutch, it's a tool – at least it should be. And as for reducing risk – well, all branding programmes involve risk and that's an issue that you have to face.

Guideline Nine – Promotion

You won't win with a brand if nobody knows about it. Most people who manage brands successfully are familiar with the mechanics of promotion. Advertising agencies, web designers, direct mail experts, public relations companies and a complex, interrelated, overlapping mass of other specialist communication organizations understand this world very well. It's all pretty familiar territory. Generally speaking, to get massive impact you have to spend massively. But like everything else to do with branding it isn't as simple as it used to be. There are lots of opportunities – working with partners on events, retailer tie-ins, co-promotions, effective use of the net – which are relatively unfamiliar or innovative and which can make the difference between powerful and weak promotion. Advertising no longer dominates in the way it once did. Successful promotion needs organization, money and collaboration.

There's an interesting corollary to all this. In *The Tipping Point* Malcolm Gladwell claims that hearsay, rumour and gossip are key in developing demand[5]. There are groups of people who lead styles which others follow. It's an interesting view, there's a lot in it and no doubt marketing people all over the world are trying to figure out who these influencers are – and how to influence them.

Guideline Ten – Distribution

Distribution is not as easy as it looks. It's certainly true that in some products and services the Internet has changed distribution patterns a lot, but in most it has just become another distribution channel – important, but not earthshattering. For distribution you want coverage.

My admired model in distribution is Disney. There is no distribution channel that Disney ignores. Every Disney distribution channel overlaps with every other. The impact is stupefying. It starts with a movie – *The Lion King*, let's say. Each major character within the film is merchandized through Disney stores, then there's the video, the musical, the book, maybe the ice show and anything else you can think of. *The Lion King* characters pop up in Disney theme parks wearing *The Lion King* costumes, some of which fortuitously may even be available for sale. *The Lion King* is serialized on the Disney TV channel. It's endless, it's ubiquitous, it's merciless – but it's effective. Not everybody can manage to do a Disney, perhaps fortunately. But every brand should think through all its opportunities to get at customers – and to reinforce its message.

To manage distribution carefully you have to be sufficiently imaginative to capture the particular audience you need. In 2002 Aston Martin, the Ford subsidiary, launched a Heritage Operation, a specially selected and carefully promoted global network as part of a 'commitment to preserve the generations of classic Aston Martins across the world'. There aren't that many new Aston Martins built – it's quite a small company – but many of the old models are still around, so many Aston Martin workshops owned and managed by Aston Martin fanatics around the world have been drawn into the network. The Heritage Operation makes friends of companies who might otherwise be competitors, and it capitalizes on customer loyalty. It is blanket coverage in its way, but the audience is small, so the blanket is as well. Very smart distribution thinking. Doesn't cost much either.

Guideline Eleven – Coherence, clarity and congruence

Finally there's coherence. All these guidelines are important but I am obsessed with coherence. In a brand the entire experience from first contact to signing off must reinforce and underline trust. Everything must fit. Every tiny piece must reinforce everything else. The brand must feel the same, wherever you touch it, or come into contact with it. Whether you are buying from it, selling to it, in partnership with it, dealing in its shares, there must be a consistency of attitude, style and culture. And this means that nothing must be out of place; nothing must jar. I have a colleague who judges organizations by the state of the toilets. She says toilets tell you everything about an organization. They tell you whether they care about detail, how hierarchical they are, whether they are modern or traditional, whether they care about their staff, whether they understand logistics issues. She's a bit of a toilet freak. But I'm inclined to agree with her.

Whenever you touch an organization – by phone or website or letter or personal visit or visit to the lavatory – it should feel the same. Plastic tea spoons don't go with Rosenthal china. All this is of course doubly true of service brands, where the key is consistent behaviour as well as consistent appearance and performance.

Only the most passionate really get it right. If you want people to believe in you, buy your shares, buy your products, understand you, recommend you to others, then you have to be consistent, coherent and credible. Only then are you in with a chance. And what makes coherence? Indoctrination. I know it's a word with sinister connotations; that's why people don't often use it. Nowadays we prefer to use more emollient words like 'training' or 'induction'. But whatever you call it, the end result is the same.

Conclusion:

Great brands get all of these things right – usually over very long periods of time. And that's why branding is nothing like as easy as it looks.

trading the

Irrespective of
ment, there is w
of the important
in the economic pe
companies. The last t
witnessed a dramatic d
between the net asset va
companies in the Standard
500 and their market capita
The aggregate market-to-boo
increased from an annual averag
around 3 at the beginning of the
1990s to a peak of 6.6 in 1999 and
2000, and still was nearly 5 after the
2000-2001 bear market.

BRANDING AND
MAKING MONEY

Everyone wants to know what their brands are
worth according to objective and respected criteria.
What's more, everyone wants to know how to pick
a winner. The thing is that only a few people can.

CHAPTER 10

I've spent much of my working life helping to create what we used to call corporate identities. In the corporate identity business, or profession as we preferred to call it, we were a bit sniffy about brands; like the rest of the world, we thought brands were what you put on supermarket shelves. We were more interested in working for the corporations behind the brands.

The corporate identity activity originated in commerce and industry with nineteenth-century industrialization. It was based around the system used by the military over centuries to create coherence and discipline and to emphasize hierarchy, precedence and order. Major programmes were created by the great railway companies whose rolling stock, stations, liveried employees and advertising were all designed to give a clear idea of the corporate attitude, style and purpose and to bond together employees in the new widely dispersed organization. Although the term 'corporate identity' was coined in the middle of the twentieth century, the

The hotel that fronts St Pancras station, London, still encapsulates the spirit of the Midland Railway brand in three dimensions long after the company itself has disappeared.

work carried out by the railway companies was the same thing under another name – corporate livery or house style. Sir John Betjeman wrote, 'The individuality of the great companies was expressed in styles of architecture, typography and liveries of engines and carriages even down to the knives and forks and crockery used in refreshment rooms and dining cars.'[1] Betjeman goes on to talk about some of the British railway companies. 'The Midland favoured Gothic, and so in a less expensive way did the Great Eastern. Greek learning dominated the London and North Western. The Great Northern went in for a reliable homeliness rather than beauty.'

The difference in personality and culture between the Midland and the Great Northern is exemplified in their two London termini. The Midland Railway's St Pancras station is one of the finest and most extravagant Victorian Gothic buildings in the world. The fantastical hotel which fronts it, designed by Sir George Gilbert Scott and opened in 1873 – 'a glorious piece of pompous window dressing'[2] was, and may once again become, when the Eurostar finally appears in St Pancras, one of the most luxurious in Europe, while Barlow's engine shed, which lies behind the station,

was, when it was completed in 1876, the largest roof in the world without internal supports. Everything the Midland Railway did in its prime was lush, extravagant and luxurious. Even its trains were designed for comfort, rather than speed.

The Great Northern, on the other hand, was 'noted more for its trains than its buildings'[3] and its terminus was at Kings Cross right next door to St Pancras. Lewis Cubitt designed and his company constructed a functional, workmanlike structure, which was completed on time and within budget in 1852. 'A superb architectural statement in its monumental plainness'[4], it could not be more different from St Pancras, its neighbour and erstwhile competitor.

Every railway company had its complement of designers, graphic artists, engineers and architects; sometimes they worked together, more often independently. Collectively their output was massive and longlasting. Even today the sad remnants of the design programmes of the different companies can still be identified poking out from the scruffy tat which symbolizes dismal Railtrack and its successor Network Rail, their down-at-heel heirs.

After the railway companies initiated these vast design programmes they were followed by shipping companies, department stores and other large and complex enterprises which needed a visual expression of coherence, discipline, hierarchy and precedence. But in the late nineteenth and early twentieth centuries the companies that appointed designers to create an overall house or visual style or corporate image were always a minority.

Most companies paid no real attention to design or, if they did, looked at it in a piecemeal fashion. For the most part buildings had no relationship with graphics, which in turn had no relationship with products – and none of it was deemed to have much relationship with sales or profitability. When banks built monumental head offices for themselves they did it mainly for self-glorification or as part of an unspoken policy of overawing their customers. The great companies of the twentieth century largely ignored or misused design. Henry Ford produced some significant cars but they weren't designed in the sense that we use the word today, and his River Rouge plant was certainly no oil painting. When entrepreneurs quite specifically took up the cause of design for its own sake, it usually became patronage in the tradition of Lorenzo de' Medici rather than Henry Ford. It was carried out for glory, not for profit.

Some of the most interesting and important manifestations of this relatively early stage of corporate identity development had a powerful social purpose. Many of the individuals who ran the few great organizations which patronized design were pioneers with what we call today a strong sense of corporate social responsibility. They wanted their staff to live and work in pleasant, well designed environments. They wanted their customers to buy high-quality, good-looking products.

Companies such as AEG wanted to create what was called in the idiom of the time 'the most intimate union between art and industry'. Allgemeine Elektricitäts Gesellschaft was established by Emil Rathenau in the early 1880s. Within twenty-five years it had become one of Germany's largest companies in the electrical field, making hundreds of products from turbines to kettles. In 1907 Rathenau and his son Walther commissioned Peter Behrens, the famous architect and designer, to be their artistic director. The appointment was announced not in the business pages but in the art column of the 28 July 1907 edition of the *Berliner Tageblatt*. On 29 August 1907 Behrens published a piece called 'Kunst der Technik' (Art in Industry) in which he described his vision at length. Put briefly it was to improve public taste. Between 1907 and 1914 Behrens and his team were commissioned to redesign buildings, products and communications material, including the corporate symbol for AEG. Behrens's associates on this vast programme included Walter Gropius, Adolf Meyer, Ludwig Mies van der Rohe and Le Corbusier, all of whom later became famous architects in their own right. The extraordinary collaboration between AEG and some of the greatest design talent of the twentieth century[5] fell to bits in 1914 at the outbreak of the First World War and was unhappily never revived, but its influence was very powerful and in some ways still resonates to this day.

AEG carried through one of the greatest commercial design programmes the world has seen and it inspired a number of other organizations. In many European countries a small but influential group of enlightened companies commissioned designers and architects to create visual identity programmes.

In the 1930s Frank Pick made London Transport into the world's most sophisticated, beautiful, modern and civilized transport system, by using the best architects and designers he could find to create an integrated, easy to use London Transport. Looking at the pitiful shambles that it has become, it seems almost impossible to believe that London once led the world's great cities in the design and implementation of a big city transport system, but it is so. And vestigial remnants of this Golden Age can be seen to this day.

London Transport in its design prime, when buildings, products and communication material all came together to project a great city transport system brand.

In Italy Camillo Olivetti and his son Adriano commissioned a design programme that was in place right up to the 1980s. Ettore Sottsass and Mario Bellini were just two of the great design consultants retained by the Olivetti company, whose policy had huge influence on design in Italy. Sibylle Kueherer makes clear that Adriano Olivetti used design for social purposes[6]. The company took great pride in the achievements of its architects and designers and celebrated their influence on and significance in the Italian world.

Until about 1950 or 1960 design, which was the root from which all this kind of work flowed, was a world apart from mainstream business. Design was in the main employed not to make profits but to demonstrate civic sense and pride. It presented the company which commissioned it as a showcase of civilized, caring modernity – an admired model, in the case of Pick beautifying the city or Olivetti showing how machines in general and office equipment in particular would enhance the quality of working

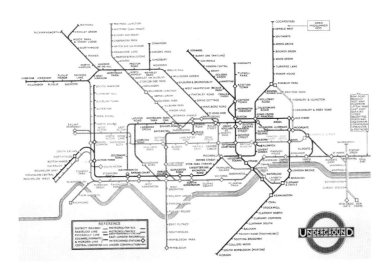

life. In the US, though, a rather different tradition had developed. There were a few companies like the Container Corporation who operated in the European tradition of general benevolence, but most were much more directly concerned with high profile, publicity and profit.

Donald Deskey, Walter Dorwin Teague, Norman Bel Geddes and others, but above all Raymond Loewy, were American designers or designers born and educated abroad who lived in America. Under the influence of that commercially driven society they first made the claim, later to become insistent and clamorous, that their products improved sales. The period of their greatest influence was the 1930s, '40s and '50s – the streamlined era. Many of these designers were showmen and self-publicists, especially Loewy, who was one of the very first designers to get into the boardroom on the basis that his work could increase profits. From Loewy's work with Gestetner, Studebaker, Lucky Strike, Shell and others, and from the less publicized but in some cases more effective work of his competitors, a new and rather separate trans-Atlantic design tradition began to emerge. Design sold things, so design was about money. That meant design could enter the business mainstream.

The phrase 'corporate identity' seems to have been coined sometime in the 1950s by Walter Margulies, of the pioneering US consultancy Lippincott & Margulies, to describe the activity in which all of the organization's visible manifestations are designed to create a coherent corporate whole associated with a specific theme, attitude or personality. The concept of corporate identity was of course directly descended from the work carried out by the AEG and before that the great nineteenth-century railway companies, but it was presented differently, much more commercially. When he worked for International Harvester and similar huge companies, Margulies took design consultancy right into the corporate heartland. Thanks partly to people like him and also to a changing commercial climate in the 1960s and more particularly in the 1970s and '80s the corporate identity discipline took off around the world, especially in the US, followed closely by Britain. The traditional European-based, designer-led visual

identity programmes with a vague and high-sounding but
rather generalized purpose mutated into systems that could help
companies to sell themselves and their products. Computer
companies, automobile companies, airlines, oil companies and
then organizations in financial services began to learn that they
could project a clear and differentiated idea of themselves to all of
their audiences, from shareholders to customers to staff, by using
visual identity systems which demonstrated their sense of purpose
or their vision. At first much of this activity was led by designers
and architects. Many of the famous names in the field at this time
were themselves designers or from a design background. Eliot
Noyes in the US, who worked for Mobil and IBM, was a classic
high-minded designer. He led IBM away from Queen Anne repro
into '60s modern on the basis that modern equipment had to
look modern. Fletcher, Forbes and Gill, a design consultancy that
mutated into the highly successful Pentagram partnership, is the
classic example of this kind of business. And as I write, happily it
still thrives. But gradually the mood changed.

Partly in order to cope with the complex requirements of their
clients, partly in an effort to learn to speak the same language, and
partly because they saw an opportunity to get closer to their clients
on a longer term basis, design consultancies of various kinds and
levels of sophistication began to employ marketing people whose
background was in commerce and industry rather than design.
These new consultants, working side by side with designers, were
educated at business schools and had MBAs. They couldn't design
but they could deal with their clients on entirely equal terms
because they came from the same business background. They
had the same disciplines and attitudes. The marketing consultants
who entered the arcane and specialized world of design began
to commercialize it. They moved on from where Loewy and his
colleagues stopped. They began to look for ways in which they
could justify their work commercially and therefore of course
their fees. This change began to take place in the '70s, as design
consultancies looked for ways of becoming more influential with
their clients. Then research of various kinds made its appearance,
leading to elaborate and often plausible rationalizations of what

was mostly intuitive work. All this changed the way design consultancies thought and acted. For the most part the design consultancies who already embraced a pretty mixed bunch – graphic designers, architects, interior designers and later new media specialists – worked quite well with the MBAs. Research and behavioural specialists also joined these consultancies, and gradually the mood and the atmosphere changed and became much more mainstream, much more business-like and profit-orientated.

Branding meanwhile which, as I pointed out in chapter 3, had traditionally been dominated by consumer goods manufacturers and their advertising agencies, also began to open up a bit. Major consumer goods companies began to use design consultancies for packaging and ranges of products because they found that specialist design companies could create more effective packaging than advertising agencies. Then they began to commission them to develop new products. Some design consultancies began to specialize in package design. Then they mutated into helping to create brands. So some of them became, sometimes slightly to their own surprise, new product development consultancies.

Then the service brands began to take off. Banks, supermarkets, petrol stations and fast food chains began to use design companies, too, to redesign their outlets in town centres and out-of-town shopping malls. These retail design consultants, who worked on interiors as well as exteriors of buildings, weren't sure if they were building brands or identities. They started to call interior design 'brand experiences'. The whole world of design consultancy began simultaneously to be permeated by and to embrace branding.

Over a relatively short time, during the decade of the 1990s, the word 'branding' came first to share equal billing with 'corporate identity' and then to displace it. Now the activity in which I have spent most of my working life is called 'branding' – and 'corporate identity' has been relegated to the slower moving world of academia. Design or identity consultants have now mostly rebranded themselves as 'branding consultants'. What they do isn't so very different from what they did before, but how they describe it is.

So now I, like many others who formerly talked about design and identity, now more often talk about brands and branding. There are both advantages and disadvantages to this semantic shift which indicate how perceptions of the whole area have changed and are continuing to change in the business world. When I first came into the design and identity field it was a sideshow. The mainstream communications world was dominated by advertising agencies. In some countries, although not so very many now, it still is. Communication meant advertising and advertising was the only form of communication that anyone knew about. Now the word 'branding' has changed all that. There isn't any doubt that branding is part of the mainstream commercial culture. In this business world branding is about making money. Branding is the real world. And advertising is part of branding – not the other way round. This means that an organization that describes itself as a branding or branding and communications consultancy is likely to be taken seriously and it may even be the lead communications supplier, supplanting the advertising agency, in a brand creation and development programme. It also means that these new forms of branding consultancy have to be multi-disciplinary. They have to embrace graphic design, new media and IT, environmental design, behavioural issues, research and all the rest of the paraphernalia. What's more, they have to be prepared to be judged on results. Their work has to perform and be seen to perform in the market place. Some of these branding consultancies have become very large. They have grown both organically and by acquisition and merger. Some became public companies, floated on the stock exchange, almost always with disastrous consequences. Most of the biggest branding consultancies are now part of global communications companies like WPP, Omnicom, Publicis or Interpublic. They are big-time mainstream businesses with offices in ten or more different countries, working with some of the world's biggest organizations in the corporate and public sector. The word 'brand' sums up what they deal in.

The drawbacks to the words 'brand' and 'branding' are, however, many and obvious. Branding implies: cosmetic, superficial, simplistic, crude and vulgar, easy to sneer at or disdain. It's still mostly associated with the supermarket shelves. On the other hand brands and branding are: quick, all-embracing, self-explanatory and suit a soundbite age. You can talk of the New York Yankees or Wharton Business School or the city of Barcelona or James Bond as a brand and everyone will understand. You can't do that so easily with identity – or even image.

'Corporate identity' has fewer derogatory associations than 'brand' but it's a bit soft and woolly. Nor is it self-explanatory. It is therefore open to every kind of interpretation and misinterpretation. Although I don't like the word 'brand' so much, I can see that it is a much more useful and more effective term.

The word 'brand' has one further huge advantage over 'corporate identity' in the commercial world, and that is that brands have direct and clear links with money, value and profitability. In the days when we all talked about identity programmes, we consultants had to struggle to demonstrate the direct and immediate connection between the work to be carried out and 'shareholder value'. Corporate identity was always associated with a whole range of factors – improving recruitment, raising morale, selling more products, reducing inventory and so on, and lots of soft issues, like being more popular and being seen to be more pleasant – but nobody that I knew attempted to put figures on it, to value it in financial terms. For the AEG, Olivetti, London Transport, Container Corporation and others of their generation it wasn't about money but social purpose. But of course if you couldn't work out what corporate identity was worth, if you couldn't put a number on it, it was quite difficult to justify. With brands there is no such problem. Brands are about making money – and they always have been. And that is the fundamental reason why the word 'brand' has supplanted all the other words – identity, image, reputation, personality and the rest of them – in the commercial world.

There is, though, a further issue. As branding expands its scope
and moves into education, charities and social foundations, the
associations with money become an inhibition. So other words
are entering the lexicon. Reputation is a more attractive and
wholesome sounding word than branding. And I think it is
quite likely that the word 'reputation' will increasingly be used
by those who regard 'branding' as too coarse and commercial to be
appropriate in describing what they do. I think it not unlikely that
some brand managers of the next generation or two looking after
universities, not-for-profits and similar institutions which reject
an overt commercial emphasis will call themselves 'reputation
managers' or something similar.

Nevertheless, as things stand today, brands and branding are part
of the tough mainstream of business, and it's therefore evident
that brands have to be worth money. 'If we're spending so much
what are we going to get out of it?' and 'What's the brand worth?'
are the questions likely to spring from the CEO's lips. Over very
many years various groups of people, mainly accountants, have
attempted to create formulae which give some kind of objective
value to brands. But there has always been a traditional bias on the
part of accountants and other valuers of corporate equity against
putting a price to intangibles. Buildings, plant, machinery and so
on are all tangible assets and therefore merit a place in the balance
sheet, and they have a value which can be more or less readily
calculated, but intangible assets like brands and for that matter
patents are harder to value. There is for example no regular liquid
market in brands.

However, since the rules of accountancy are above all flexible, and
since it's clear that all kinds of intangible assets like brand and
patents and other forms of intellectual property are becoming
increasingly significant, accountants are beginning to challenge
their own rules.

Brands themselves have over some years changed hands for large
sums of money. A lot of sensible companies have paid good money
for them so there must be some way of valuing them. That is why a

number of organizations are setting themselves up both to value brands, to try to create a place for them in the balance sheet and generally to tame them so that they can fit into the corporate structure in a fashion that is apparently logical, rational, methodical and above all susceptible to numerical analysis. In other words the new idea is to create a formula to value brands both on the balance sheet and within the corporation.

Although there have been discussions around the balance sheet value of brands for many years the change of mood has taken place since the early 1990s when there was a 'dramatic divergence between the net asset value of the companies in the Standard and Poor's 500 and their market capitalization. The aggregate market to book ratio increased from an annual average of around 3 at the beginning of the 90s to a peak of 6.6 in 1999 and 2000 and still was nearly 5 after the 2000-2001 year market.' I derive this quotation from BrandEconomics of New York, a company that was set up in 2002 with the express purpose of valuing brands, quantifying the relative importance of brands across industry sectors, and advising on growth opportunities for branding, all in an apparently rational and rigorously numerical series of formulations. The BrandEconomics system is not the first but it is the most comprehensive, inventive and persuasive formula for valuing brands that I've come across. To my no doubt cynical and jaded mind it comes over a bit like the principles of scientific advertising so popular in the 1920s. It's the nearest thing I've come across to doing brand management by numbers – literally. Consultancies that create these formulaic systems claim to reduce the risk in creating and sustaining brands. I doubt it. Removing creativity doesn't remove risk. It compounds it.

The Orange brand is worth a lot of money.

Of course it's important to put a value on brands if you can. And of course it's important to reduce risk. But the truths around the brand are both simpler and more complex than the mathematical intricacies suggest. You don't need a complex formula to work out the value of a brand. A brand is simply worth what anyone is prepared to pay for it. As I have suggested again and again in this book, where there is increasing competition in the market place

and where this is linked to increasing similarity of performance, in other words where innovation doesn't create significant, long-term competitive advantage, branding becomes overwhelmingly important because it becomes the major, sometimes the only, differentiator. Where this happens and customers pay more over a consistent period of time for what they know and what they like, then branding is seen to work – and that's why successful brands are worth a lot of money.

No financial formula, however apparently all-embracing, is going to help significantly in creating and sustaining brands. All it will do is help some of the less self-confident people working on brands feel better. They can also say it wasn't their fault if things went wrong, because they were only following the rules. No doubt these complex and rational-seeming financial formulae will sell well to organizations lacking self-confidence and self-belief and to people within them wanting to guard their backs. Everyone wants to know what their brands are worth, according to objective and respected criteria. What's more, everyone wants to know how to pick a winner. But only a few people can. Creating brands involves risk and is largely intuitive. So these financial formulae for calculating brands seek to quantify the unquantifiable. No doubt, though, the many marketing people and chief executives who are unable to choose a shirt in a store without a great deal of creative assistance will find that the application of the principles laid down by BrandEconomics and its peers greatly assists them in what they hope will pass for creative decision taking. You could say, if you felt like being cynical, that peddling statistics of dubious value to the profoundly unimaginative and unconfident will provide a pretty good living for a lot of clever people, even though it may not help very much to create successful new brands or revive sad, old, declining ones.

And of course it's all based around numbers. Numbers are the talisman of our age. They justify everything. It must be true because the numbers say so. I am always amused and sometimes amazed by the way in which numbers, sometimes tendentious, frequently torn out of context, occasionally quite meaningless and arbitrary, are used to give a false but nevertheless comforting air of verisimilitude to even the most evident rubbish. Numbers form the basis on which far too many decisions are justified by executives – especially those involved in marketing. And the more apparently precise the numbers are the better. 68% is better than 70%. And 68.4% is even better. It's more exact and therefore more credible. How many people stop to ask themselves whether it's really 68.4% rather than a substantial majority? Many numbers are false and misleading. It's perhaps worth remembering that two of the greatest brand successes in recent years – Baileys and Orange – did pretty badly with the numbers when they were originally researched and before they were put on the market.

It starts at business schools. In most business schools I have been involved with, numbers are elevated to mystical if not mythical status and instinct, initiative, feelings – all of those factors which cannot be quantified but on which our lives are largely based – are relegated or devalued or dismissed as unquantifiable and therefore inadmissible. Bearing in mind that we make the most important decisions in our lives around our feelings – who we love, who we marry, who we hate, where we live, what we believe in – then you might regard the mythologizing of numbers as a bit out of proportion, even unbalanced, but that's business (and business schools) for you. The real issue underlining all this is creativity and next to it is chance, and the unpredictable nature of the human condition and the human psyche. Numbers diminish these. They give an executive an entirely false sense of security. They may even make him or her feel numbers are in charge.

I'm not even beginning to suggest that numbers aren't important or that they aren't vital in the management of any business. It is the apparent precision of numbers in business life that creates the problem. Many numbers are ludicrously unreliable as the financial scandals of Enron and others in 2002 made clear. The *Economist*, a pretty dab hand at numbers itself, had this to say about different accounting systems: 'A company's earnings under American accounting rules, for example, can be twice as high as under British rules without any bending at all.' Numeracy is a very important component in business life but it isn't the only component. Instinct, experience and judgment also matter. Luck, serendipity, brilliance, experience and courage play a major part.

So with the intervention of formulaic number-crunching brand advisors, what is happening to brand consultancy? Several things. First, many advertising agencies are looking for ways of regaining the high ground of branding, by setting up strategic branding units inside their own businesses. Some of them are doing well at this and regaining business from the specialists.

Second, brand consultancies are getting bigger – merging, acquiring each other and in turn being acquired by the major communication groups who dominate the industry – so that they become global businesses with a full range of disciplines. Many of these organizations are enthusiastically embracing the numbers-based formulae of branding, because it seems to provide comfort and reassurance to the more conservative and perhaps more bewildered and less self-confident of their clients.

Third, and I suppose inevitably as a reaction to the development of orthodoxies, a newish breed of brand consultancy is developing, formed sometimes from people who have worked in other creative businesses – music, the arts or journalism. Many of these new consultancies ignore all of the structures, disciplines and systems that have emerged over the years; they are simply creative hot shops. In other words they hark right back to the design consultancies that worked in the 1930s right up to the 1980s. In 2002 Tyler Brûlé of Wink Media, who created the highly successful magazine *Wallpaper**, was appointed to design the identity of Swiss, the airline that arose from the ashes of the old Swissair. He beat a number of well established brand consultants to get the job. Many of the more courageous large companies experimenting with new brands or new ways of doing things with old brands are using these new consultancies.

So what's going to happen? The numbers brigade will continue to crunch their dreary way through to greater influence. Most branding work will therefore be banal and mundane. But simply because of this, the lively creative groups both big and small, old and new, will be seen to be producing the cleverest, freshest and most successful work and the more courageous, smarter, quicker organizations will employ them. We seem to have seen some of this before.

STOP

E$$O

GET ACTIVE ON
SATURDAY 18TH MAY

To organise your own family-friendly
Stop Esso Day event or to join an existing one
visit www.stopesso.com or call 0870 010 9510

Whatever you do, don't buy Esso –
they don't give a damn about global warming

GREENPEACE Friends of the Earth people & p

BRANDS: **WHO IS REALLY IN CHARGE?**

The solutions lie with us. We have to be alert to the way brands behave and misbehave. We have to reward the good ones with our loyalty and punish the bad ones by avoiding them.

CHAPTER 11

PREVIOUS PAGES
Esso, the Exxon Mobil
brand environmental
activists love to hate.

Brands from companies are getting stronger and they are proliferating. Some are even taking over the companies that spawned them. They are becoming more insistent and clamorous. Brands are amoral in their lust to outsource at the lowest cost and sell at the highest price. They are intent on becoming ubiquitous as they move from one country and one continent to another, ignoring or overwhelming venerable ethnic, cultural and religious traditions. Brands are increasingly disingenuous and duplicitous in their relentless pursuit of our money and they will stop at nothing in their overwhelming imperative to manipulate us. It doesn't make any difference to them whether we are young or old, rich or poor, can or cannot afford to buy, or even whether we want what they offer, brands are after us and we have to stop them.

This, broadly speaking, is the argument made by the Naomi Klein school of brand critics who take the view that the commercial brand is out to take us over completely and if we're not careful it will. It's anti-globalization and anti-big business. It's a very seductive line of argument but it exaggerates commercial branding's strengths and ignores its weaknesses. You need to examine brands and the corporations that own and control them very carefully to find out what's really going on, and then see how paying customers react to brands, how pressure groups have influenced them and how a high-profile public position has made them vulnerable.

The brand is very largely the corporation's tool. When the corporation has problems, when it is perceived to be deceitful, greedy, dishonest, heartless or incompetent, the brand suffers. But in addition to the corporate issues with which it is lumbered, the brand also has its own problems. Although from the outside some brands may look as though they are conquering the world, all brands are always insecure.

First, brands are vulnerable to fashion. Fizzy drinks like Coke and Pepsi are now being attacked by stimulation drinks like Gatorade. The entire fast food industry is also being threatened because chronic obesity, which is endangering health both in the

US and some European countries, is increasingly being blamed on McDonald's and its competitors. As I write this in 2003, McDonald's is being sued by lawyers representing overweight children, and its expansion plans are on hold[1]. It seems likely that fashions in foods are changing and salads and other 'lite' foods are becoming more popular.

Second, brands are vulnerable because they get too cocky and arrogant and think they know best. Gap, Levi's and Marks & Spencer have all learned that lesson the hard way.

Third, brands are vulnerable because, despite all the research and the focus groups, the people who create and manage brands can't really anticipate how people will use them. Not one single cell phone company anywhere in the world anticipated the growth of texting. In April 2002 5.2 billion text messages were sent[2]. Texting has become one of cell phones' most lucrative and attractive services and nobody forecast it. The new 3G cell phone technology is a huge gamble; nobody has any idea how or even if it will take off. There are many similar examples. Range Rover was the first of the Sport Utility Vehicles. It was brilliant conceptually but it has spent its entire lifespan struggling to keep up with just those trends that it serendipitously inspired.

Fourth, brands are vulnerable because they don't seem to be able to anticipate changes in public opinion. Look at the fast food industry again or the row over genetically modified foods, which I'll return to later.

Finally, brands are not only vulnerable to the public's whims, they also spend a great deal of time, energy and money fighting each other. Competition between them is murderous. Adidas and Nike are now on top. Puma (with Serena Williams) is catching up. Mastercard, Visa and Amex are scrapping it out. Diners is still there but you wouldn't notice. Fiat, for over a hundred years Italy's greatest brand, is now on the danger list. In the UK retail market, C&A, a major High Street name, disappeared round the turn of the millennium although it's still going strong elsewhere in

Europe. If you think about it you can name plenty of big brands that have just expired.

In other words, brands are nothing like as powerful as they look. They are particularly vulnerable to us, the customers. When we like them we buy them. When we don't we walk off. Customers can be loyal, fickle, slaves to fashion, creators of trends or all of these simultaneously or serially. Above all customers are unpredictable. We do what we feel like. In addition, the brand is part of the corporation. What the corporation does and how it behaves has a direct and powerful impact on the brand. And when you start adding the corporation's problems to the brand's you can see that brands don't have it all their own way. Not by a long chalk.

What companies get up to is now a matter of major public concern. As Rufus Olins, Editor-in-Chief of *Management Today* puts it, the private life of a company isn't private anymore. The rules of business are changing and companies are being pushed and chivvied – often by pressure groups – into taking a new and more responsible position. Virtually everything the corporation does can be and often is subjected to detailed scrutiny.

The privatization of telecoms, health, transport and so on has made companies central to our everyday lives. Many of the basic activities that the state used to run are now managed by private companies. Recurring crises in food such as the BSE scandal, or in transport such as rail disasters, or in the financial sector such as pension fraud and balance sheet lies, remind the public that huge mistakes get made and barefaced deceptions are practised and often, quite rightly, companies get the blame.

As we have already seen, companies are also loosening their ties with the nations from which they originate. Globally, companies now have the ability to shop around for the best deals in terms of business conditions, taxes and regulations when deciding where to produce or invest. They can open factories and reduce unemployment or close them and contribute to it. They can stay in a country or move away from it. This means that they are often

perceived to be in the driving seat in their relationships with
national governments, so members of the public, consumer
groups, environmental groups and the media demand that
that power is combined with responsibility, and they scrutinize
companies and their brands as never before, at the same time as
financial pressures on shareholder value continue to intensify.

The pressures on companies come from two directions, both of
which contain massive internal contradictions: the first pressure
relates to corporate behaviour, corporate social responsibility, the
stakeholder society and similar matters. Here the rules are getting
stricter and behaviour that used to be ignored is now often
questioned or even vilified. The requirement to behave better
means bigger overheads and this in turn means that companies
can either pass on higher prices to the customer or accept lower
profits. But it seems that while we customers like companies to
behave nicely, we aren't always so willing to put our money where
our mouth is and pay more. So companies are facing a double bind.

Take outsourcing: companies have always looked for the cheapest
place they could produce goods at the quality they wanted. So they
went to countries where labour was cheap and almost inevitably
conditions of work were poor. If suppliers used child labour or
treated their workers inhumanely that wasn't the company's
problem. Nike, Gap and the others never gave it a second thought.
They weren't the first companies to use cheap labour, they just
followed traditional practices. If they thought about it at all,
they could claim that their suppliers treated their employees no
worse and sometimes better than local companies. In the event,
to their credit, pressure groups alerted the public to some of the
exploitation that outsourcing can engender. Companies with big
brands are now learning that suppliers have to be supervised
carefully, and their staff treated as part of the global family. If
they aren't, suppliers' behaviour could shame and humiliate their
global partners. A recent *Sunday Times* article offers a fairly typical
example[3]: under the headline 'Top Shops use Europe's Gulag
Labour', the article reads 'Marks & Spencer, C & A, Debenhams and
Laura Ashley are among companies using factories where workers

are fainting at their machines.' This sort of publicity terrifies companies, undermines their brands and very properly makes them modify their stance. In other words, increased transparency leads to much more responsible corporate behaviour. A highly desirable outcome, no doubt.

But are we prepared to pay for it? The jury is out. Oxfam, a British-based charity, along with others, started Fairtrade in the 1960s. It was a scheme that guaranteed producers in developing countries a decent price for their products. In 2001 ethical groups, including Fairtrade, had $11.5 billion worth of sales in the seven food and non-food segments in which they operated[4]. Although this only amounts to 1.5% of that market place Fairtrade is growing fast – double the growth rate of non-ethicals, according to the Co-op Bank's Ethical Purchasing Index.

Fairtrade does not expect customers to buy only out of sympathy or charity. It operates on the assumption that only if price and quality are competitive will emotional factors start to operate. The more successful Fairtrade becomes the greater the budget for branding.

Although it's early days and Fairtrade is still a tiny player in the market there are some hopeful signs. The UK Co-operative Group, a major retailer with a market share that has been declining for decades, sees Fairtrade as a significant differentiator. And they may be right. In the emotional muddle that often swamps us when we buy, feeling good about ourselves must have some significance. Despite all this, though, most successful retailers – Wal-Mart, Aldi and Tesco – will tell you that price is a dominant factor.

The row over genetically modified foods is much more complex but also involves price. Experts take very different views. So far as a lay person can judge, the arguments against GM foods and supplements are unproven and yet, because of various public health scares, which are not necessarily even directly related to the GM issue, and egged on by pressure groups, ill-educated, half-informed public opinion is demanding that everything should be organic. It's clearly desirable to put pressure on the food industry – from growers right through to manufacturing and distribution chains – to raise standards, to look at factory farming, ill treatment of animals, modification of seeds, labelling of products and so on, but to demand 'organic' products (will 'barn-fresh' do?) as a kind of catch-all answer is a bit naïve. And you can't have higher quality food without paying more for it. But consumers are notoriously stingy. They don't want to pay more, not if they can avoid it, with a more or less clear conscience. They let Mom and Pop corner stores go out of business because they charge more and stock less than supermarkets and then they blame Wal-Mart or Tesco for killing them. These two contradictory pressures really bewilder companies. The issue is clear: the higher the standards, the higher the price. Will customers, led by pressure groups to demand higher standards, be prepared to pay more? Although it's not proven, so far it doesn't look like it. Maybe pressure groups should try harder with consumers.

The second set of issues relate to financial integrity, greed, fraud, fiddling the books and so on. Society has always been suspicious of businesses and ready to pounce on fraudulent behaviour. Anthony Trollope's *The Way We Live Now*, starring a corrupt financier, was written in 1871. Charles Dickens's *Martin Chuzzlewit* features the tragi-comic fraudster Monty Tigg, who sometimes attempts rather thinly to disguise himself as Tigg Montagu. Historically there have always been companies that have behaved fraudulently so there's nothing much new in the spate of corporate wrongdoing revealed in the scandals of 2002. But now there's an extra pressure – the frenzied rush for short-term profit to get higher share price. The actions of WorldCom, Enron and others of course is repulsive and inexcusable, but in the wild corporate financial climate created by the financial markets it's hardly surprising. The pressure from financial markets for what they insist on calling 'shareholder value' drives companies towards juggling with the numbers in order to achieve, or at any rate pretend to achieve, astronomical rates of growth. If shareholder value – or more bluntly short-term share price, based around ludicrously ambitious growth targets, linked to senior employee stock options – is the sole criterion by which a company's success is judged by the financial community, some companies are inevitably going to play dirty. And, of course, if you start playing fast and loose with corporate numbers there's a strong temptation to do the same on a personal level.

So in addition to being model corporate citizens, going organic, selling products cheaper than anyone else and sometimes even trying to give decent service, companies are also pushed by the financial markets to deliver record profits – 15% to 20% increase year on year, which is pretty near impossible. How can every company grow at 15% or 20% per year when the economy is growing at about 2% to 3%? GE, for at least a decade the world's most successful company, promised growth at 18% per year and appeared to deliver it. If GE had continued at that rate, in one hundred years it would have taken over the world. It now transpires that GE didn't deliver 18% growth per year. GE delivered about 9%, but financial juggling contrived to make it look bigger. 9% per year is actually pretty good but it wasn't quite what GE's management had promised. Enron and WorldCom also got themselves tied down to delivering huge increases in profits year on year. These were of course linked to executive bonuses which ordinary wage earners found grotesque. Neither company could hit these targets because they were impossible to achieve. So in an atmosphere of lunatic vainglory that they themselves had helped to create they fiddled the books. This isn't to excuse but partly to explain what happened and why. And it hardly needs pointing out that all this doesn't do the corporation's brands any good.

So, what with one thing and another, corporations are having a tough time adapting to a new high-profile role. How do companies deal with public controversy? How do they try to reconcile the demand for better behaviour, higher quality products, cleaner balance sheets and much higher profits with the equally strong demand for lower prices? Mostly, pretty ineptly. For the most part they are simply out of their depth. They do not know how to deal with demands that are stuffed with internal contradictions and they don't fully understand the public implications of their actions. They know they have to react to the contradictory pressures they face but they aren't quite sure how. And while big business seems to sense that the rules are changing, it doesn't yet know what the new rules are. Businesses are finding immense difficulties in reconciling the conflicting demands placed on them. They keep on making a mess of their corporate public relations because much of the time they don't know what to do in the contradictory climate in which they operate, nor are they bold enough to say things they know are true, like if you want it organic – truly organic – it won't be cheap. And what's more, it probably won't look so pretty, even though it may taste better and be good for your health. Or if you want us to develop new life-saving drugs, cures for hideous diseases like Parkinson's and multiple sclerosis, there might have to be some animal testing. And if at the same time you sustain an unrelenting pressure on short-term profitability and shareholder value, the chances are that some businesses are going to cut corners. In other words, many companies are defensive, evasive and shifty because they are bewildered. They are also, perhaps not surprisingly, cynical, because they sense that the buying public want the highest moral standards, which they aren't prepared to pay for, while shareholders – some of whom must also be customers – demand the highest possible profits, and these things are simply not compatible. I know some wise people at the top of companies who are fully aware of these double standards and the hypocrisy that accompanies them, but they are reluctant openly and publicly to say what they really think because of the impact it might have on sales or share price.

It's a bizarre phenomenon that companies which are so sophisticated at promoting their brands are frequently so naïve at a corporate level. Many of them can't even deal with a product failure without botching it up. Coca-Cola may be able to influence children and young people all over the world to buy its sugary liquid confection in ever increasing quantities, but the company has signally failed to deliver the same level of expertise in its corporate communications. Can you really believe that Coca-Cola the brand, with its hugely expensive, farsighted and clever promotional techniques, derives from the same company that made such a shambles over its product failures in Belgium in 1999? Some batches of Coca-Cola were contaminated because a bottling plant in Antwerp used the 'wrong' carbon dioxide to put fizz into soft drink bottles. A number of people became ill. It was terribly unfortunate, but these things occasionally happen. Nobody died. So why hide it? Why deny it? Why try to ignore it? All simple mistakes novice crisis managers would tell you not to make. Coca-Cola made all of them. The Coca-Cola Corporation could hardly have performed worse in this crisis if it had tried. But this isn't unusual. In reality global corporations, however smart they may seem to be with promoting their brands, are still for the most part slow, clumsy and defensive when they deal with the media corporately. Despite all of the lessons from PR consultancies about 'crisis management', business doesn't really know how to deal with public criticism. Business people could, and no doubt will, eventually learn a lot from politicians, whose public life is one long crisis, but they still have a very long way to go. Their first reaction is denial rather than explanation or apology. They seem shifty even when they have nothing to hide.

In the longer term, of course, these public pressures which so unnerve corporations are good news because they persuade them to behave more responsibly. But they do lead to confusion, uncertainty and caginess. Despite what it might look like from the outside, companies and brands are not marching forwards conquering everything that lies before them. They are not bamboozling customers all over the world into buying any old rubbish they feel like churning out, even though they might like to. On the contrary, for the most part they are shambling around in circles trying to find a way through the mass of paradoxes, contradictions and double standards that being increasingly important, influential and under constant scrutiny has created for them. And as they do so they explore different routes.

In each sector you will find corporations exploring different directions. Take the oil industry, one of the world's largest and most influential sectors. Within the oil world – a global business where size matters – the impact on environmental issues is really

significant, geo-political debates are at the heart of the activity
and the public profile of individual companies is very high. The
major players are tackling this new high-profile, highly critical
world in different and contrasting fashions. Shell and BP are
playing the role of the politically correct goodies and Exxon
Mobil is acting out the simple tough guy. The three companies
are the biggest in the business. Each has grown aggressively, BP
and Exxon Mobil mainly by acquisition, Shell mainly organically.
Their different postures illustrate ways in which companies are
reacting to current challenges.

As an Anglo-Dutch company which operates around the world,
Shell is much more experienced in operating across cultures than
most other global companies. It has learned a lot from the costly
mistakes that badly damaged its reputation in Nigeria and over
Brent Spar. Shell has embarked on a major process of social and
environmental reporting, informal consultation mechanisms with
its staff and a new appraisal system intended to make community,
social and environmental work a valued part of job performance.
In other words, Shell is trying to behave itself better all over the
world. This faces the company with very difficult and potentially
costly options. In exploration, for instance, should it try to get
the oil out fast and cheap and maybe damage the environment,
undermine indigenous cultures, tacitly co-operate with guerrillas
or authoritarian governments and then take the public
consequences if its behaviour is exposed, which was the way oil
companies operated before people started poking their noses in?
Or should Shell follow a different path? Bear the extra costs of
extraction but behave in a socially and ethically responsible way:
this means not doing deals with insurgents, taking care of the
environment, taking time to work with the local community in
education, health, employment, policing and related matters, and
accepting that the oil will cost a bit more per barrel to extract?
These aren't easy choices – especially when you're operating in a
volatile market place where price per barrel is key. Shell says it's
going to do things the right way. It's going to play by the rules.
Its new, much-trumpeted and so far as I can judge quite sincere
attitude, despite the fact that it is regarded with some scepticism

by its more traditional managers, is accompanied by a campaign around the world which explains this rather belated conversion. The Shell Report of 1998, *Profits and Principles: does there have to be a choice?*, encapsulates the global company's attempts to talk soft, to emphasize its sense of responsibility to society as a whole and its new willingness to listen – Tell Shell.

As I outlined in Chapter 5, BP is even more forthright in its overt commitment to sustainable environments and every other form of political correctness. Like Shell, BP operates in a highly competitive, aggressive global market place with competitors and partners who are not necessarily particularly finicky in sticking to the ethical rule book. BP seems quite determined to become an exemplar of model behaviour. But it isn't easy to change and old habits die hard. On balance, though, despite a few slips here and there, when you take everything into consideration, BP is doing rather well in its new role.

Exxon Mobil, on the other hand, regards BP and Shell's behaviour and attitudes towards corporate social responsibility, environmental sustainability and all the rest of it as pathetic wimpish hogwash. Exxon Mobil has cast itself in a John Wayne role. It represents rugged individuality and the American Way. It has a robust, not to say aggressive attitude to its critics. It operates in the real world where men are men, oil is oil, and whatever gets in the way can take the consequences. It supports opposition to the Kyoto Protocol which calls for cuts in green-house gas emissions and it claims that its critics exaggerate and don't truly understand the issues that they are demonstrating against. In other words it prides itself on being an old-fashioned advocate of the view that profits and shareholder value come first, medium and last, and all the other stakeholders come nowhere. But Exxon Mobil is in danger of becoming the brand you love to hate. The real issue for the company is whether, if enough customers don't like the way it behaves, they'll go somewhere else, and the company will notice it. So far, despite a lot of bad publicity Exxon Mobil continues to perform well financially and boycotts have had little effect.

The two wholly contradictory postures of BP and Shell on the one hand and Exxon Mobil on the other illustrate the current corporate dilemma. These companies are at opposite ends of the spectrum on issues of corporate responsibility and behaviour. The reality is that in the face of a changing, volatile and uncertain public climate in which customers' behaviour is still unpredictable there is, as yet, no common corporate view. Attitudes and behaviour vary from one company, one brand, one industry, and even one country to another.

An increasing number of companies are attempting to legitimize themselves – to become a respected part of the fabric of society – a bit like Shell. These organizations are just beginning to comprehend the immense scale of the issues involved. They are beginning to realize that legitimizing yourself is not just about obeying the law; it is about anticipating it, policing yourself and your suppliers, and being ready to justify your activities in terms of their overall social impact. The real test will come when public opinion is sufficiently mobilized by pressure groups to create boycotts on a significant scale. If nobody bought fuel from Esso stations in Europe for just one month, it would have a dramatic impact on Exxon Mobil's policy and behaviour, but so far at any rate public awareness of these issues is patchy and inconsistent.

It appears to me that you can divide current corporate attitudes to these matters into three broad groups. The first group, like Shell and BP, take their social responsibilities seriously. At the other end of the spectrum, the second group follow the Exxon Mobil model. They regard these issues as petty and irritating distractions from their principal concern, which is to maximize profits. They may pay some cosmetic lip service to environmental sustainability but that's about as far as it goes. Currently, so far as I can judge from the board rooms with which I am familiar, this is the view of the majority of the big companies. It's changing but slowly – and they could certainly do with a push. So a bit of action from anti-capitalist pressure groups might help move things along. The third and last group is stuck somewhere between the two extremes. These are companies that are well disposed to all of these issues but do not regard them as having a high priority. They know they will probably have to do something sometime but they don't know what or how or when. My observation is that companies belonging to this group won't move till some disaster threatens them or someone in their world. I am clear, however, that over the next few years the second and third groups will shrink and the first, the active proponents of good corporate behaviour, will grow and dominate the corporate world, but only when public opinion is sufficiently mobilized to hit companies hard in their pockets when they misbehave. The point is simple. Companies will embrace social responsibility when it is in their long-term financial interest to do so.

In the meantime a new growth industry is developing around the idea of corporate social responsibility, abbreviated into the initials CSR. In its most radical manifestation CSR seeks to harness the corporation's organizational, creative and cultural capabilities to make the world a better place. In *Good Business*[5] the authors Steve Hilton and Giles Gibbons, who run a social marketing company called Good Business (what a coincidence), describe a range of projects, mainly undertaken by their clients. These companies range from home improvements businesses who work with suppliers of 'well managed forests' in Papua New Guinea, thereby getting higher quality timber, giving a better and more sustainable living to forest workers and improving transport and community links, to Sky TV's funding a social initiative in giving careers advice to drifting teenagers under the banner headline 'Reach for the Sky', with the central message 'See what you can be'. In the world of 'Good Business' companies don't get involved in CSR in order to be seen to be behaving properly; they do it because they genuinely want to improve society. Well, maybe.

Inevitably this new interest in CSR has led to some quite comic and rather unlikely developments. For example, the British American Tobacco group – probably quite sincerely – engages in CSR activities around the world. In Kenya BAT supports small business; in Malaysia it supports students looking for higher education, and so on. This leaves CSR consultancies, of which there are of course a growing number, with a dilemma. Should they help to turn the baddie into a goodie or should they not sully themselves by association? The CSR issue turns much more farcical when well known corporate scoundrels suddenly present themselves as angels. Some British high street banks – and they know who they are – hitherto far from distinguished by their benevolent attitude towards their own customers and staff, let alone society as a whole, have also undertaken CSR activities. I owe to my colleague Slawa Shumowski the thought that this kind of breathtaking hypocrisy is reminiscent of the Soviet Union in its prime, when the reality of life and the propaganda produced by the state bore absolutely no relationship to each other. The wisest thing such organizations could do, if they genuinely embrace concepts around CSR, is to act quietly and with a certain discretion – even, dare I say it, humility, at least until the bad odour surrounding them disappears. As the post-Second World War British Prime Minister Clement Attlee is reputed to have said to the loquacious political philosopher Harold Laski, 'A period of silence on your part would be welcome.'

Leaving aside the jokers in the pack, Hilton, Gibbons and many others for that matter see CSR emerging as a serious theme in corporate life. And they are right. Why? Because of enlightened self-interest. Other things being equal, companies that are seen to behave well will be more successful in the longer term than companies that don't bother. Inevitably, though, in the short and medium term CSR brings lots of problems and paradoxes. It's an interesting thought that Body Shop, started by the maverick Anita Roddick in 1976, has always embraced CSR. For a number of years Body Shop was regularly hounded by financial analysts for its social policies; either it wasn't putting profits first or it was hypocritical because it was pretending to embrace social causes just to get cheap publicity. The business world found it difficult to believe that Roddick meant what she said and that CSR could go hand in hand with business success. All that has now changed. Body Shop is vindicated. Now most major companies are trying to copy her.

Only a few companies are built like Body Shop around the CSR idea. For most incorporating it into the culture is difficult. Who runs CSR? How do you reconcile it with maximizing profitability, shareholder value and old style 'tooth and claw' capitalism? Is it something the corporation does quietly or is it part of the changing public face of the enterprise? And how do the corporation's brands, which are inevitably their most high-profile activity, associate themselves with these issues? Nobody really knows the answers yet.

All of which brings us back to McDonald's and the horrors revealed in Eric Schlosser's *Fast Food Nation*[6]. McDonald's is one of the world's most famous and most successful brands, although it has been having a relatively difficult time since around the turn of the millennium. Because it is so high profile and so public, McDonald's should be a model of excellent corporate behaviour. But apparently it isn't. Schlosser reports that most of the major fast food retailers, including McDonald's, tolerate dangerous and exploitative behaviour amongst their suppliers and that they are prepared to accept unhygienic products made under revolting conditions. If Schlosser's account is to be believed we put our health at risk every time we walk into McDonald's and many other fast food outlets.

Schlosser then goes on to make the point that attentive readers may have noticed more than once in this book, which is that we consumers have the ultimate power over corporations. We can make them behave the way we want them to. 'Nobody in the United States is forced to buy fast food,' says Schlosser. 'The first step towards meaningful change is by far the easiest: stop buying it. The executives who run the fast food industry are not bad men. They are businessmen. They will sell free-range, organic, grass-fed hamburgers if you demand it. They will sell whatever sells at a profit.'

There is no ducking out of this. If we as consumers don't like the way companies behave we can walk away from them. And then they will change in the way we want or they will die. It's not branding as such that's a problem, nor is it big companies, nor globalization, nor any of the other bogey men that the anti-capitalists throw stones at. The real problem is public apathy and private greed. If we are content as consumers to allow companies to behave badly, cut quality, exploit their workforce, then many, certainly not all, but anyway plenty of them will. What's more, if we think lower prices are more important than higher quality, decent treatment of animals and an out-of-control agrochemicals industry, then that's what we'll get. Because in a capitalist society profit matters most and the less a product costs and the more it sells for, the higher the profit and the greater the shareholder value.

So the solutions lie with us. We, the public, we consumers, have to be alert to the way companies and their brands behave and misbehave. We have to reward the good ones with our loyalty and punish the bad ones by avoiding them. If we can't be bothered to do that, we will get what we deserve.

It isn't, then, a question of simply attacking corporations and their brands, although I'm all in favour of exposing malpractice, and in this respect many pressure groups do a great job. It's about being selective, making it clear that the reward for good behaviour is something every company understands. And that is higher profits.

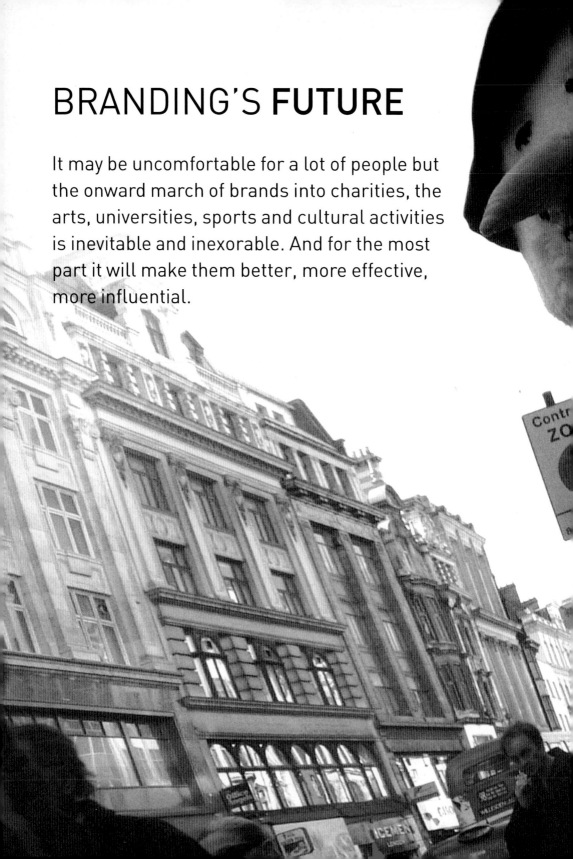

BRANDING'S **FUTURE**

It may be uncomfortable for a lot of people but the onward march of brands into charities, the arts, universities, sports and cultural activities is inevitable and inexorable. And for the most part it will make them better, more effective, more influential.

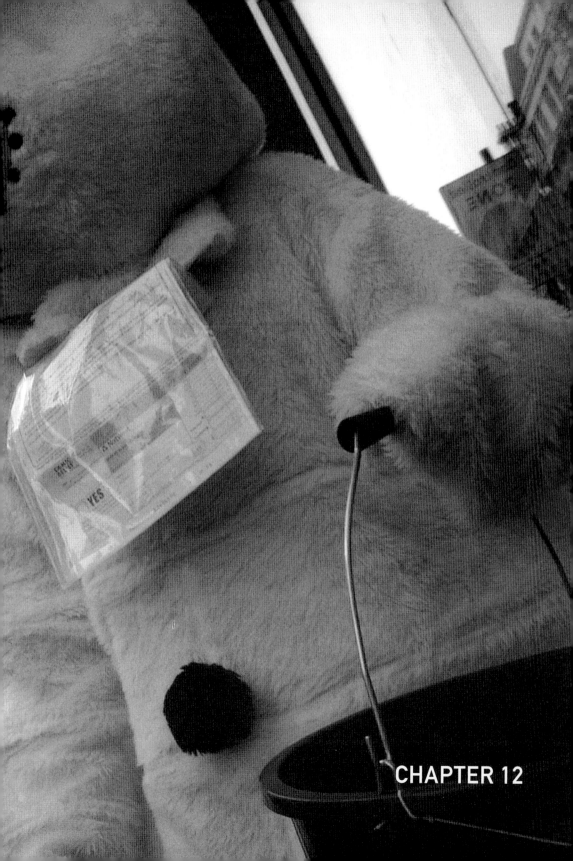

CHAPTER 12

PREVIOUS PAGES
Red Nose Day in London, 2003. A charity initiative that the public likes.

Inevitably, I suppose, the bulk of this book has been concerned with brands in a commercial context because that is where they are at their most formidable. Branding in sport, the arts, education, charities and social foundations is for the most part much younger and is certainly more fragile. Although there are some outstanding and highly sophisticated examples – Real Madrid, Juventus and Manchester United in soccer, Tate in its various manifestations in art, Insead and Harvard amongst business schools, WWF in charities – these remain for the moment relatively unusual. But branding techniques are now entering the non-commercial world and we can expect them to spread like wildfire – because branding works.

OPPOSITE
Some manifestations of the Tate brand.

Take cities. The world is now awash with competitions for Cities of Culture and Cities of Architecture and Design. The competition for the European Capital of Culture has been trotting around from one country to another, carefully avoiding offending national sensibilities since 1985. In 2003 six candidate cities, reduced from twelve, competed for the title. Cardiff estimated the potential economic benefits at $1.64 billion. Inverness reckoned success would add a third to tourist numbers in the Highlands of Scotland. Newcastle suggested its victory would create 17,500 jobs and at least $1.15 billion in economic benefits[1]. Liverpool won. The economic fallout looks good. All kinds of figures have been bandied about: 14,000 jobs, $3.3 billion in investment, an extra 1.7 million visitors. Glasgow, which was Britain's last European Capital of Culture in 1990, dates the beginnings of its transformation from a junkyard of decaying engineering industry to a vital, creative hub with an impressive, home-grown culture and a lively tourist industry from that time. In 1999 it was City of Architecture and Design, which gave it another major boost.

None of the cities in the competition is mentioning the dirty word 'brand', but that of course is what it's all about. The success of Bilbao, Barcelona, Graz and Glasgow, to name just a few cities that have dramatically changed their reputations by changing the reality while simultaneously making prodigious efforts to change perceptions, has set the example. Before the Guggenheim Museum opened in 1997 the only people who visited Bilbao were sailors

from the ships that docked there, and they had nowhere else to go. Since 1997 the Guggenheim Museum has attracted 5 million visitors. In its first three years it generated $500 million in economic activity and $100 million in new taxes.

In December 2002 Shanghai won the competition to host the 2010 World Expo. According to the *Financial Times*, the city 'approached the event as a brand-building exercise'[2]. The *FT* goes on to say, 'It invested millions to win the bid, even taking out full page advertisements in international newspapers on the eve of the vote.' Shanghai beat Moscow and other tough customers. The city expects 70 million Chinese and foreign visitors to its six-month world fair. The intention naturally is that Shanghai's efforts in the 2010 Expo will complement those of the Beijing Olympics in 2008 and help change world attitudes towards China. All this is an echo of what the Seville International Expo and the Barcelona Olympics together achieved for Spain in the 1990s.

Exhibitions and world fairs are largely a nineteenth-century invention. Beginning with Prince Albert's Great Exhibition of 1851 in Hyde Park, London, such forums became a very familiar way of boasting about national achievements and of putting the cities in which they were held on the world stage. Subsequently there were a lot of American fairs – Philadelphia Centennial in 1876, San Francisco in 1915, Chicago in 1933 and the New York World Fair in 1939 – but the French were really masters of the genre. They held one expo after another, each with its own architectural influence. The Eiffel Tower was built for the Exhibition of 1889. Art Deco came of age with the Paris Exhibition of 1925 called 'Arts Decoratifs et Industriels Modernes'. Nowadays branding cities is quite as high on the agenda as branding nations, about which I have written at some length in Chapter 8. So, as usual, when we look back a bit we find little that is really new.

Branding, then, is moving into nations, regions and cities. Where else is it going? Well, one of the places to look is the social sector. This is increasingly being described as the Third Sector. It comprises a complex web of organizations principally defined by the fact that they do not exist to make a profit. Museums, orchestras, art galleries and universities are all part of it. So are charities. The word 'charity' has a multiplicity of associations often related to do-gooding endeavour, dedicated, badly paid full-timers, ill-trained, enthusiastic part-timers, all mixed up with ideas based around nineteenth-century philanthropy and twenty-first-century social responsibility and justice. Charities are also bound up with shoe-string budgets, make do and mend and a rather messy Scotch tape management culture. The offices of a charity should, it seems, look poor, rundown and shabby; the people who work in them should look drab. Incompetence in matters of organization is an accepted hallmark. Charities are perceived as a bit depressing and low calibre. Traditionally, being a bit bedraggled is the admired model. It must be the case that somewhere deep down inside them, this is the way charities have wanted to be. Looking and acting shabby emphasizes their own sense of being worthy and worthwhile. This may be an unfair and exaggerated picture, but it isn't wholly inaccurate. And although there are plenty of national charities and now even quite a number of global charities, the majority remain local and narrowly focused. I've spent many years as a consultant working with charities and my experience has been that they are often unreasonably demanding with no real feeling for priorities. Everything is equally important, so you can't get a clear brief. On top of all that the lower the fee the more difficult, demanding and woolly-minded they seem to become. And if you work for nothing they give you a really bad time. So my experience of most charities is that they have been good to keep away from.

But there have always been exceptions. Some charities have always been highly focused, well structured, very disciplined, heavily branded and very well marketed. And not always the newest. The Red Cross was founded by Jean Henri Dunant, a Swiss, after he had seen the horrors of the Battle of Solferino in the Franco-Austrian War of 1859. Its position as a completely neutral global agent for the relief of every kind of human affliction is unassailable. The Red Cross manages its brand superbly. Its symbol must be one of the best recognized in the world. Equally interesting, although smaller and somewhat more quirky in many

Red Cross, perhaps the most easily recognized brand in the world.

ways, is the Salvation Army founded by William Booth in Victorian London. Booth was a fervent Christian who had seen London's poverty at very close hand. He had written about the life of the labouring classes, about their problems of drink, prostitution, incest, filth, overcrowding and other horrors. As a result of these experiences and in an attempt to bring Temperance and God to the poor he founded what eventually became the Salvation Army.

From the very beginning the Salvation Army was heavily branded. It was based around the military model – the admired model of its time. Its members, both men and women, wore distinctive uniform, as they still do, and they had quasi-military ranks. Its journal was called the 'War Cry'. Its staff instructions were called 'Orders and Regulations for Field Officers'. The Head of the Army had the rank of General. Salvation Army chapels were called Citadels; some of them had crenellated walls like mock medieval castles. Uniformed Salvation Army brass bands played jolly hymns ('Why should the devil have all the best tunes?' asked Booth rhetorically) outside pubs to rescue the fallen from the evils of drink. Like the best brands, the Salvation Army went global. It currently has operations in over one hundred countries. The Salvation Army is a significant and quite remarkable charitable global brand. Under a thin disguise it features in the great American musical *Guys and Dolls* as the Save-a-Soul Mission. The Sally Ally, which still flourishes, inspired a number of imitations and became a model for other quasi-military brands.

The Boy Scout movement founded by Lord Baden-Powell, the Hero of Mafeking, owed something in its branding policies to the Salvation Army. A global not-for-profit organization concerned with the training, upbringing and welfare of boys, the Boy Scouts also have uniforms, titles, tests and a complex vocabulary all of their own; 'jamboree' and 'toggle' are distinctly scouting terms. The paraphernalia of scouting exercised a huge influence over the imagination of boys from all over the world for generations. Together with their siblings, Brownies, Guides and Cubs, the heavily branded Scouts represented for virtually the whole of the twentieth century a significant part of the Third Sector. Unlike the Red Cross or the Salvation Army, who seem to have continually adapted themselves to changing behaviour patterns, the Boy Scout movement failed to reinvent itself over time. It did not adapt to contemporary culture. As a result, sadly, the brand itself is now a struggling anachronism.

The Third Sector, then, is not new. In fact it has existed for over a century in a variety of forms. But it is currently growing fast and developing a high profile. The reasons for this are complex, but principally they relate to the inability of governments to sustain their traditional social roles. In health, education and even prisons, governments are abdicating their position simply because they can't afford the expense. It is this vacuum that the Third Sector is filling.

The charity sector has taken on a new lease of life. There are a lot of relative newcomers. Many charities, such as Amnesty International, Christian Aid, Médicins Sans Frontières, Red Cross, Children's Aid, World Vision, Greenpeace, Friends of the Earth and WWF, have professionalized themselves. They have become or are becoming world-class brands. They have a powerful point of view. They campaign for funds vigorously and effectively. They have readily recognizable names and symbols which they protect ferociously. The WWF fought a running battle with the World Wrestling Federation over the use of its initials, which it seems to have won. Branding in the context of charities and for that matter other parts of the Third Sector, too, can become a formidable tool. Sometimes, as in commercial entities, a powerful, outspoken individual makes a difference. Under the charismatic Des Wilson, Shelter, a charity for the homeless in Britain, emerged from obscurity into headline news. Wilson exploited the media to bring the plight of the homeless to the public's attention. It was an extraordinary achievement led more or less by one man. And that was back in the 1970s when the climate was much less favourable and commercial organizations were much less involved in corporate social responsibility.

Today it is quite usual for charities to be involved in significant joint branding operations with commercial entities, for example Greenpeace with Timberland and Christian Aid with WorldCom. But they have to be careful. Christian Aid may have backed the wrong horse. Bernie Ebbers, the driving force behind WorldCom and a man who calls himself a committed Christian, has not emerged with entirely clean hands as WorldCom collapsed through massive financial fraud around his ears, but maybe the collateral damage, as the military put it, hasn't done too much damage to Christian Aid. Benetton has teamed up with the World Food Programme in a campaign called 'Food for Life'. According to the *Guardian*[3], 'The WFP, which feels that it cannot spend money on paid advertising, approached Benetton precisely because of its reputation for "sensitising public opinion to issues".'

In any event the requirement for large companies to display a social conscience and for charities to professionalize themselves and piggy-back on the energy, effort, promotional sophistication, distribution and wealth of commercial brands appear happily to coincide. Over the next few years we can expect to see far more charity and big company relationships established, some even on a permanent or semi-permanent basis. And this will mean that charities will learn how to manage themselves more effectively and how to adapt branding methodologies to suit their own conditions and purposes.

Charities will be fewer, bigger and more consequent. Currently there is a vast proliferation of them. Almost everywhere you look, you fall over one. There are about 87 children's charities alone in the UK. Barnardo's, NSPCC, Children's Aid are some of the bigger ones. Some of these overlap with others; some have particular niches in mental or physical illness or abuse or special needs. They are all no doubt worthy, but few individually possess the organizational and promotional skills or the money to develop effectively by themselves. What's more, having 87 charities with 87 names, 87 offices, 87 sets of overheads however minuscule, 87 sets of promotional material mostly of a banal nature (how many plastic pens can you use?), all competing with each other, is not only messy, but more important it's highly inefficient, wasteful and counter-productive. And it doesn't help the children in need. How can members of the general public make sense of this? How can we distinguish between one children's charity and another? How can we have the faintest idea what happens to our money? How can a charity, having once captured our interest, sustain it so that we remain regular, committed and brand loyal? For the most part, the answer to all this is that charities don't deal with these issues in a professional way. With a few outstanding exceptions, like Barnardo's, it all seems rather ad hoc and amateur. But it needn't be.

It won't go on like this in the longer term. Business techniques will take over – mergers, amalgamations and takeovers. The mutation of charities into sophisticated national and global players is inevitable. The natural concomitant of this is branding. Over the first quarter of the twenty-first century branding will become a powerful force in charities. Major charities will capture our concern and interest and our money. They will draw us into Friendship Associations and try to tell us how our particular donations are used. They will become skilled at merchandizing their clothing and memorabilia. They will memorialize us. They will create headlines out of heartbreaking cases which will engage us and persuade us to commit money and sometimes time to their cause. They will link us to individual cases, personalize it all. This kind of commitment to charities will enable us to feel better about ourselves.

There is nothing nasty or sinister in any of this. Aid, charity, redistribution of wealth through means other than those for which the state is usually deemed responsible will become increasingly important over the next few decades. In this new sector, halfway between the worlds of government and business, or between public worlds and private, what we now clumsily call not-for-profit organizations will become increasingly powerful, as they take over roles previously managed by central or local government. Branding, adapted from the commercial world, will help this sector to become more efficient and effective.

And it isn't only charities that will emerge. Housing associations which sit half-way between the public and private sectors are a classic example of the kind of Third Sector organizations that will become much more important. As I write, social housing which has traditionally been created, managed and funded by local government in many countries in the Western world is increasingly being taken over by housing associations which are funded jointly both by the public sector and by financial institutions like banks. Housing associations increasingly provide not just housing, they also create neighbourhoods with a range of amenities including schools, playgroups and shops. They can create employment and can help in neighbourhood regeneration. But housing associations are currently not well known and their activities are not generally understood by the various publics with whom they deal. They have often operated as small, local units without a clear voice or remit; they have been tools of national policy over which they have no influence or control. Now in England housing associations, through their trade association the National Housing Federation, are creating a brand which is intended to give them a clear national voice, which will explain what they do and become a base from which to influence developments in their sector. This brand will enable them to gain recognition and to take control of their own destiny.

Education – particularly university education – is another area which will look to professional branding techniques for help. The gulf between privately and publicly funded institutions of higher education is now widening. In the US, privately funded universities are, with a few exceptions, the richest, the most successful and the most prestigious. In other parts of the world, where publicly funded universities are very short of money, going private is once again becoming a real option for some. But it's a big risk. You can't go private successfully unless you can raise the funds. Privately funded universities like Harvard and Stanford are successful because they attract money. And they attract money because of their reputation. Competition between institutions of higher education is intense. Those universities with the best reputation attract funds and therefore the best academic staff and high achieving students. They also do the best research. The brand with the best reputation wins.

University reputations usually rise and fall quite slowly – over many years. But there is no doubt that they do change and reputation management, or as we might put it more coarsely, brand management is becoming increasingly important for them.

Almost every major university has now woken up to the issue of competition and most are beginning to understand, as industry learned in the 1970s and '80s, that to win in the race they don't just have to be better than their competitors, they have to be seen to be better. Universities are also beginning to realize that they don't just have to be as good as Harvard; they also have to show that they are different – that they have attitude. So, almost inevitably, universities are embracing branding.

As the private sector moves in, competition will get tougher. Take Oxford, one of the best known university brands in the world. Oxford has one of the finest and most advanced medical faculties around and is a leader in technology transfer activities but it still has a reputation for the humanities based around dreaming spires, punting on the Isis and strawberries and cream, all based on a world created by Evelyn Waugh and perpetuated in Colin Dexter's 'Inspector Morse' series. Its reality has changed but perceptions remain locked in the past, and because Oxford is so very well known it's hard to bring perception in line with the current reality.

As in so many commercial brands, the university brand is a mix of product, communication, behaviour and environment. Product, of course, is key. High levels of teaching and research, and a good sprinkling of Nobel Prize winners, are a prerequisite for a world-class institution of higher education and research. But communication, especially with alumni who are often potential donors, is also very important. American universities never lose sight of this. Their alumni network is based on the simple reciprocal assumption that you've taken from us and now you have to give back. American universities attract huge sums from their alumni.

Environment also plays quite a large part in the perception of institutes of higher education. The University of Virginia, for example, has a sublime campus and it also enjoys a good academic reputation. Maybe if the campus wasn't quite as good the reputation wouldn't be either. A beautiful environment can't completely outweigh an inferior or obsolete product, however, and Salamanca in Spain can't hide long-term decline despite its staggeringly beautiful site. Nor does a low calibre environment always inhibit recognition of a superb product. The Massachusetts Institute of Technology is not graced by a beautiful campus, but the product excellence shines through. Looking good helps, though. And where universities build new, they often try to get the best architects to build award-winning buildings, in which they emphasize the donor's name – Said Business School at Oxford is a classic example. Just like cities; for example the Guggenheim in Bilbao.

'Pay your taxes,' says this brochure, produced for the Serbian government in 2003.

When you start thinking about it broadly, almost all the limitations to branding fall away. In very many parts of the public sector the same story emerges. Look at a revenue service or a police force. Both of them largely depend for their success on levels of public co-operation. If, as in some countries, culture dictates that people who pay taxes are deemed to be foolish, then most people will evade taxes until the culture is changed. Perhaps the entire Italian revenue service needs to be rebranded and reorganized. Mind you, that might be true of the Italian civil service as a whole.

Each police force depends for its success on the level of public co-operation that it achieves. And that in turn depends on its reputation. If the police are regarded as a bunch of corrupt and brutal thugs, licensed to extort because they have a uniform, they can't expect and they won't get much public co-operation. As I commented in Chapter 9, the critical factor in the brand mix for a police force is the behaviour of individual officers in their day-to-day relations with members of the public. But although a police service is a behaviourally dominated brand, product, communication and environment also matter. Police stations, for example, are mostly intimidating places. They need to be more open, friendly and neutral. A more thoughtful and open approach to the interaction between police and members of the public would help.

In all the sectors I've just so cursorily looked at, the issues that I examined in the introduction to this book are being played out. Each sector has a technical or craft skill base, a financial skill base and a seduction or brand skill base. Inevitably, because of their origins, craft skills have almost always predominated. The people who inspired, created and built up charities, housing associations, orchestras, theatre companies, museums, art galleries, universities, and for that matter police forces, too, have always cared above all about what they did. They were craftsmen first. They did it because they wanted to. Because they thought they had something to give. They felt they had talent and a vocation. And it's right that they should have felt these things. But the time is coming when seduction skills will become as important for these organizations as technical or craft skills. If they want funding, high-quality staff, a good customer base, respect, even admiration from the community, they will increasingly have to consider the mechanisms of branding – or, if you prefer, reputation-building. Over the next decade or so, as techniques of fund-raising and presentation become increasingly significant, branding will take another huge leap.

The battle between the financial, technological and seduction skills that has been played out in companies is now just beginning to emerge in these new sectors. The days when a chairman of a charity could be openly contemptuous of branding are over, or they soon will be. It may be uncomfortable for a lot of people but the onward march of brands into charities, the arts, sport and culture is inevitable and inexorable. And for the most part it will make them better, more effective, more influential.

What does all this mean for the societies in which the people of the richer countries in the world live? In a sense it is rather odd that so many people feel emotionally involved with products and services as superficial and intrinsically trivial as soft drinks, hamburgers and running shoes. If branding can, in its strange, illogical, emotional way, encourage people to develop a close rapport with products like these, what will it be able to do when its power is released for genuinely significant and worthwhile activities?

The real issue here is what kind of a society do we want? Do we want to continue to live in a world in which the individual distinguishes himself or herself from others almost exclusively through what he or she owns and therefore displays, or is there at least some possibility that many of us will wish to reinforce our own sense of identity by associating ourselves with areas of long-term value like the arts or education? Already many people show an intense dedication and loyalty to sport. Might some of us not feel more content with our own sense of self if we were seen to be associated with giving and being seen to give to cultural and socially valuable institutions, rather than simply flaunting the baubles of commercial product and service ownership? This raises huge issues about greed, envy and the nature of capitalism and the consumer society. Personally I cannot believe that simply wanting more provides ultimate satisfaction. I am quite as greedy for products as most people, but after a bit, like many people, I suspect, I get a little fed up with trinkets.

There is or there should be a lot of emotional satisfaction in giving. Very rich people have always given. The Ford Foundation, the Rockefeller Foundation, the various Carnegie, Nuffield and Wolfson institutions and thousands of other truly useful organizations throughout the world have been founded and funded around the instinct of rich people to donate in order that they can feel both emotionally content and to preserve their own names for posterity.

We live in a world in which many millions of people are very rich by the standards of previous societies and many more millions are very well off. The mechanisms to persuade the mass market rich to contribute are still pretty undeveloped. Third Sector institutions have not yet understood how to persuade and seduce the quite but not very rich to spend their money on activities that bring immense personal, emotional satisfaction and that can also contribute collectively in a massive way to the continuing improvement of our society. I am convinced that there is a vast opportunity here. Branding as clever, sophisticated and sensitive as that applied in commerce and industry can make this happen and can maybe even help to change the world. We can all be persuaded to be proud to contribute.

In the longer term, then, the role of brands in society will be exactly what we want to make it. Branding has given commerce immense power and influence; it can do precisely the same for the arts, sport, health, education and other social areas, and for the welfare and well being of the underprivileged and vulnerable all over the world. Branding outside commerce can fulfil a major social purpose, if we want it to.

We love brands because they make life more attractive and easier and because we define ourselves through them. We like their complex mix of function and emotion. We like the way they complement and manifest our personality. We like brands that help us to say something about ourselves. We have the power to shape brands to be what we want and to shape the society in which we live.

All we have to do is use that power, and use it for mutual benefit.

NOTES

Introduction
1 Bryan Burrough and John Helyar's truly gripping book *Barbarians at the Gate: The Fall of RJR Nabisco* (Harper & Row, New York, 1991) describes in detail this kind of corporate culture.
2 See Naomi Klein, *No Logo: Taking Aim at the Brand Bullies*, Picador, New York, 2000

Chapter 1 Why brands are important to customers
1 Jean-Noël Kapferer, *Strategic Brand Management: New Approaches to Creating and Evaluating Brand Equity*, Free Press, New York, 1994; one of the leading textbooks on marketing
2 James B. Twitchell, *Lead Us Into Temptation: The Triumph of American Materialism*, Columbia University Press, New York, 2000. Twitchell teaches English and Advertising at the University of Florida.
3 *Financial Times*, 19/20 April 2003

Chapter 2 How VW, the ultimate craft-based company, fell in love with brands
1 Walter Henry Nelson, *Small Wonder: The Amazing Story of the Volkswagen*, Little, Brown and Company, Boston, rev. ed. 1967

Chapter 3 Where brands came from – and what happened when they grew up
1 Mark Pendergrast, *For God, Country and Coca-Cola: The Definitive History of the Great American Soft Drink and the Company That Makes It*, Basic Books, New York, 2nd ed. 2000; a fascinating study
2 Charles Wilson, *The History of Unilever: A Study in Economic Growth and Social Change*, Cassell, London, 3 vols, 1954 and 1968
3 ibid.
4 ibid.

Chapter 4 Living the brand – managing service brands
1 *Financial Times*, 5 November 2001

Chapter 5 Brands on a global stage – homogeneity, heterogeneity and attitude
1 *Wall Street Journal*, 8 August 2001
2 *Financial Times*, 5 November 2001
3 See Peter Drucker, *Economist*, 3–9 November 2001
4 From a promotional card in the bar of the Mirabelle restaurant, Mayfair, London, November 2001

Chapter 6 Why brands are important inside companies – bonding as much as branding
1 *Economist*, 10 January 1998
2 *Financial Times*, 20 October 2002

Chapter 7 'Made in…' What does it mean and what is it worth?
1 *Financial Times*, 5 September 1998

Chapter 8 Branding the nation
1 Dominic Lieven, *Empire: The Russian Empire and its Rivals*, John Murray, London, 2000; a magnificent book
2 ibid.

Chapter 9 How to create and sustain a brand – some guidelines
1 *Financial Times*, 5 November 2002
2 See Per Mollerup, *Marks of Excellence: The History and Taxonomy of Trademarks*, Phaidon, London, rev. ed. 1999
3 *Economist*, 6 April 2002
4 This point is clearly expressed by Richard A. Normann in his excellent book, *Reframing Business: When the Map Changes the Landscape*, John Wiley & Sons, Chichester, 2001
5 Malcolm Gladwell, *The Tipping Point: How Little Things Can Make a Big Difference*, Little, Brown & Company, Boston, 2000

Chapter 10 Branding and making money
1 Sir John Betjeman, *London's Historic Railway Stations*, John Murray, London, 1972
2 From David Atwell's chapter in *Railway Architecture*, ed. Marcus Binney and David Pearce, Orbis Books, London, 1979
3 Sir John Betjeman, op. cit.
4 David Atwell, op. cit.
5 This is celebrated in *Industriekultur: Peter Behrens and the AEG, 1907–1914* by Tilmann Buddensieg in collaboration with Henning Rogge, MIT Press, Cambridge MA, 1984
6 Sibylle Kueherer, *Olivetti: A Study of the Corporate Management of Design*, Rizzoli, New York, 1990

Chapter 11 Brands: who is really in charge?
1 In a jokey piece (but terrifying for McDonald's) the *Economist* compared the company's plight with tobacco companies and suggested that within a decade (say, 2012) McDonald's might be in big trouble with litigation.
2 *The Oldie*, July 2002
3 *Sunday Times*, 26 September 1999
4 *The Observer*, 2 February 2003
5 Steve Hilton and Giles Gibbons, *Good Business: Your World Needs You*, Texere, New York and London, 2002
6 Eric Schlosser, *Fast Food Nation: The Dark Side of the All-American Meal*, Houghton Mifflin, Boston, 2001

Chapter 12 Branding's future
1 *Financial Times*, 28 October 2002
2 *Financial Times*, 11 December 2002
3 *Guardian*, 14 February 2003

BIBLIOGRAPHY

al-Khalil, Samir, *The Monument: Art, Vulgarity and Responsibility in Iraq*, Andre Deutsch Ltd, London, 1991

Alter, Peter, *Nationalism* (2nd ed.), Edward Arnold, London, 1994

Anderson, Benedict, *Imagined Communities: Reflections on the Origin and Spread of Nationalism*, Verso, London, 1983

Barman, Christian, *The Man Who Built London Transport: A Biography of Frank Pick*, David and Charles, Newton Abbott, 1979

Barnes, Julian, *England, England*, Picador, London, 1999

Barthes, Roland, *Elements of Semiology*, Cape, London, 1984

—, *Mythologies*, Cape, London, 1973

Bellow, Saul, *Ravelstein*, Viking, London, 2000

Bennet, E. A., *What Jung Really Said*, Schocken Books, New York, 1988

Boilerhouse Museum, *Coke*, 1986

Braudel, Fernand, *The Perspective of the World*, Fontana Press, London, 1985

—, *The Structures of Everyday Life*, Weidenfeld & Nicolson, London, 2002

—, *The Wheels of Commerce*, HarperCollins, London, 1982

Campbell, Joseph, *The Hero With a Thousand Faces*, Princeton University Press, Princeton, 1949

Colley, Linda, *Britons Forging the Nation 1707–1837*, Pimlico, London, 1992

Cox, Howard, *The Global Cigarette: Origins and Evolution of British American Tobacco, 1880–1945*, Oxford University Press, Oxford, 2000

Crampsey, Bob, *The Empire Exhibition of 1938: The Last Durbar*, Mainstream, Edinburgh, 1988

Davies, Norman, *Europe: A History*, Oxford University Press, Oxford, 1996

De Chernatony, Leslie and Malcolm H. B. McDonald, *Creating Powerful Brands*, Butterworth Heinemann, Oxford and Boston, 1992

Diamond, Jared, *Guns, Germs and Steel: The Fates of Human Societies*, W. W. Norton, New York and London, 1997

Dixon, Norman F., *On the Psychology of Military Incompetence*, Cape, London, 1976

Featherstone, Mike, *Consumer Culture and Postmodernism*, Sage, London, 1991

Ferro, Marc, *Colonization: A Global History*, Routledge, London, 1997

Fombrun, Charles J., *Reputation: Realizing Value from the Corporate Image*, Harvard Business School, Boston, 1996

Forty, Adrian, *Objects of Desire*, Thames & Hudson, London, 1986

Gellner, Ernest, *Nationalism*, Phoenix, London, 1997

—, *Nations and Nationalism*, Blackwell, Oxford, 1983

Goodchild, John and Clive Callow (eds), *Brands, Visions and Values*, Wiley, Chichester, 2001

Greenhalgh, Paul, *Ephemeral Vistas: The Expositions Universelles, Great Exhibitions and World's Fairs 1851–1939*, Manchester University Press, Manchester, 1990

Hayward Gallery, *Art and Power: Europe under the Dictators*, South Bank Centre, London, 1995

Heskett, John, *Philips: A Study of the Corporate Management of Design*, Trefoil, London, 1989

Hirsch, Fred, *Social Limits to Growth*, Routledge and Kegan Paul, London, 1977

Hobsbawm, E. J., *Nations and Nationalism since 1780: Programme, Myth, Reality*, Cambridge University Press, Cambridge, 1990

— and Terence Ranger (eds), *The Invention of Tradition*, Cambridge University Press, Cambridge, 1983

Horne, Donald, *The Great Museum: The Re-presentation of History*, Pluto Press, London, 1984

Horsman, Mathew and Andrew Marshall, *After the Nation-State: Citizens, Tribalism and the New World Disorder*, HarperCollins, London, 1994

Ignatieff, Michael, *Blood and Belonging: Journeys into the New Nationalism*, Vintage, London, 1994

Jung, C. G., *Man and his Symbols*, Aldus Books in assoc. with W. H. Allen, London, 1964

Kedourie, Elie, *Nationalism* (4th exp. ed.), Blackwell, Oxford, 1993

Kellas, James G., *The Politics of Nationalism and Ethnicity*, Macmillan, Basingstoke, 1991

Kennedy, Paul, *The Rise and Fall of the Great Powers*, Fontana, London, 1989

Kiernan, V. G., *Imperialism and its Contradictions*, Routledge, London, 1995

Landes, David S., *The Wealth and Poverty of Nations: Why Some are So Rich and Some So Poor*, Little, Brown and Company, London, 1998

Leonard, Mark (ed.), *The Future Shape of Europe*, The Foreign Policy Centre, London, 2000

MacKenzie, John M., *Propaganda and Empire: The Manipulation of British Public Opinion*, Manchester University Press, Manchester, 1984

Naisbitt, John, *Global Paradox*, Nicholas Brealey Publishing, London, 1995

Norbye, Jan P., *The Complete History of the German Car*, Random House, London, 1988

Opie, Robert, *The Art of the Label*, Simon & Schuster, London, 1987

—, *Rule Britannia: Trading on the British Image*, Viking, London, 1985

Papanek, Victor, *Design for the Real World*, Thames & Hudson, London, 1972

Pavitt, Jane (ed.), *Brand.New*, V&A Publications, London, 2000

Pfaff, William, *The Wrath of Nations: Civilization and the Furies of Nationalism*, Simon & Schuster, New York, 1994

Porter, Michael E., *Competitive Advantage*, Free Press, New York, 1998

Ridderstrale, Jonas and Kjell Nordstrom, *Funky Business*, ft.com, London, 2000

Samuel, Raphael (ed.), *Patriotism: The Making and Unmaking of British National Identity Vol. II, Minorities and Outsiders*, Routledge, London, 1989

— (ed.), *Patriotism: The Making and Unmaking of British National Identity Vol. III, National Fictions*, Routledge, London, 1989

— and Paul Thompson, *The Myths We Live By*, Routledge, London, 1990

Saxton, Joe, *Polishing the Diamond*, nfpSynergy, 2002

Schama, Paul, *The Embarrassment of Riches*, Fontana, London, 1988

Seton-Watson, Hugh, *Nations and States: An Enquiry into the Origins of Nations and the Politics of Nationalism*, Methuen, London, 1977

Sloan, Alfred P., *My Years with General Motors*, Penguin, Harmondsworth, 1986

Trevor-Roper, Hugh, *Princes and Artists*, Thames & Hudson, London, 1976

Trompenaars, Fons, *Riding the Waves of Culture: Understanding Cultural Diversity in Business*, Nicholas Brealey Publishing, London, 1993

Wells, H. G., *Tono-Bungay*, Macmillan, London, 1908

White, Richard, *Inventing Australia*, Allen & Unwin, Sydney, 1981

Wiener, Martin J., *English Culture and the Decline of the Industrial Spirit 1850–1980*, Cambridge University Press, Cambridge, 1981

Williams, Gareth, *Branded? Products and their Personalities*, V&A Publications, London, 2000

Zola, Emile, *Au Bonheur Des Dames (The Ladies' Delight)*, Penguin, Harmondsworth, 2001

—, *La Débâcle (The Debacle)*, Penguin, Harmondsworth, 1972

PICTURE CREDITS

ACKNOWLEDGMENTS

I've lived with many of the ideas that I've attempted to express in this book for many years, but it's taken a bit of time for them to mature. Many of my thoughts derive from discussions with friends, colleagues, former colleagues, students, clients (some of whom are also friends) and family, and I'd like to thank them all for putting up with me.

I don't suppose this list of acknowledgments includes everyone but I hope it takes into account most people. If there are other people who made a contribution and have not been thanked, and I'm sure there are, I'm very sorry I haven't mentioned them, and I'd like to thank them too.

My particular thanks to Jacob Benbunan, Brian Boylan, João Miguel Braz-Frade, Carlo Brumat, Bill Castell, Jesus Encinar, Edwina Finlay, Winston Fletcher, Philip Gibson, Marcus Gregson, Mary-Jo Hatch, Stephen Hayward, Cyrus Jilla, Jonathan Knowles, Suzanne Livingston, Rufus Olins, Juan Pablo Ramirez, Rafael Ramirez, Paul Rogers, Joe Saxton, Majken Schultz, Slawa Shumowski, Angela Wilkinson, and especially Dornie Watts.

Jane and Richard Wentworth produced many of the witty pictures.

Daren Cook designed the book and took many of the pictures with his usual extraordinary mix of passion, flair, professionalism and speed, and I am most grateful to him.

I'd also like to thank my former colleagues at Wolff Olins for generously letting me have access to data and my present colleagues at Saffron for being so accommodating about my various foibles.

I'm a difficult mixture of conscientiousness and untidiness. Working with me must be at best difficult and at worst ghastly so I'd like to thank Jane Houghton and Simone Fletcher with whom I started this project and Lisa Ahrens who has worked on it to the bitter end. They have all typed, retyped, researched, adjusted, changed, modified and modulated it. I can't thank them enough – especially Lisa.

Despite all the arguments, discussion and advice that I've had, some of which I've taken, naturally I take full responsibility for all the opinions expressed in the book.

Wally Olins
Goring-on-Thames,
Oxfordshire, 2003

INDEX